WRITING 21ST CENTURY FICTION

HIGH-IMPACT TECHNIQUES
FOR EXCEPTIONAL STORYTELLING

DONALD MAASS

WD
WRITER'S DIGEST
BOOKS

WRITER'S DIGEST
BOOKS

An imprint of Penguin Random House LLC
penguinrandomhouse.com

ISBN 978-1-59963-400-5

Printed in the United States of America

Edited by Roseann Biederman
Designed by Claudean Wheeler
Illustrations by aggressor/Fotolia.com

DEDICATION

For Abi

whose 21st century story is mysterious,
beautiful, and ours

ACKNOWLEDGMENTS

My thanks to my wife Lisa Rector-Maass, and my colleagues at Donald
Maass Literary Agency who held the fort: Jennifer Jackson, Cameron Mc-
Clure, Charles Noyes, Amy Boggs, Jennifer Udden, Stacia Decker, Katie
Shea, Emily Gref, and Rachel Kory.

Huge appreciation also to Kelly Messerly, Suzanne Lucas, Roseann
Biederman, Kate Travers, Jessica Strawser, Chuck Sambuchino, Phil Sex-
ton, Brian Klems, and everyone at Writer's Digest for their expertise and
ongoing support.

Reverent homage to Therese Walsh and Kathleen Bolton of Writer
Unboxed.com, where many of the ideas in this volume were first introduced.

Trembling gratitude to the coffee bars of the West Village where much
of this book was written: in particular Bakehouse, Grounded, Minerva,
and Mojo.

ABOUT THE AUTHOR

Donald Maass heads the Donald Maass Literary
Agency in New York City, which represents more
than 150 novelists and sells more than 150 novels
every year to publishers in America and overseas.

He is a past president of the Association of Authors'
Representatives, Inc., and is the author of several books, including *Writing the Breakout Novel* and *The Fire in Fiction*.

NOTE

This book is an analysis of advanced fiction techniques, including examples from a diverse selection of recent novels. In the pages ahead you will find enormous plot spoilers. If you prefer that your reading retain its surprises, first read the novels listed here.

NOVELS EXCERPTED

From *Garden Spells* by Sarah Addison Allen, copyright © 2007 by Sarah Addison Allen, published by Bantam Dell, a division of Random House, Inc.

From *The Stormchasers* by Jenna Blum, copyright © 2010 by Jenna Blum, published by the Penguin Group, Penguin Group (USA) Inc.

From *Rainwater* by Sandra Brown, copyright © 2009 by Sandra Brown Management Ltd., published by Simon & Schuster

From *Changes* by Jim Butcher, copyright © 2010 by Jim Butcher, published by ROC, New American Library, a division of Penguin Group (USA) Inc.

From *Little Bee* by Chris Cleave, copyright © 2008 by Chris Cleave, published by Simon & Schuster Paperbacks, a division of Simon & Schuster, Inc.

From *The Hunger Games* by Suzanne Collins, copyright © 2008 by Suzanne Collins, published by Scholastic, Inc.

From *The Last Detective* by Robert Crais, copyright © 2003 by Robert Crais, published in the United States by Ballantine Books, an imprint of The Random House Publishing Group, a division of Random House, Inc.

From *Loser's Town* by Daniel Depp, copyright © 2009 by Daniel Depp, published by Simon & Schuster

From *Revolution* by Jennifer Donnelly, copyright © 2010 by Jennifer Donnelly, published in the United States by Delacorte Press, an imprint of Random House Children's Books, a division of Random House, Inc.

From *Gas City* by Loren D. Estleman, copyright © 2007 by Loren D. Estleman, published by Tom Doherty Associates, LLC

From *Extremely Loud & Incredibly Close* by Jonathan Safran Foer, copyright © 2005 by Jonathan Safran Foer, published by Houghton Mifflin Harcourt

From *The Hotel on the Corner of Bitter and Sweet* by Jamie Ford, copyright © 2009 by James Ford, published in the United States by Ballantine Books, an imprint of the Random House Publishing Group, a division of Random House, Inc.

From *A Reliable Wife* by Robert Goolrick, copyright © 2009 by Robert Goolrick, published by Algonquin Books of Chapel Hill, a division of Workman Publishing

From *The Magician King* by Lev Grossman, copyright © 2011 by Lev Grossman, published by Viking, an imprint of Penguin Group (USA)

From *gods in Alabama* by Joshilyn Jackson, copyright © 2005 by Joshilyn Jackson, originally published in hardcover by Warner Books, an imprint of Warner Books, Inc.

From *An Affair Before Christmas* by Eloisa James, copyright © 2007 by Eloisa James, published by Avon Books, an imprint of HarperCollins Publishers

From *Torment: A Fallen Novel* by Lauren Kate, copyright © 2010 by Tinderbox Books, LLC and Lauren Kate, published in the United States by Delacorte Press, an imprint of Random House Children's Books, a division of Random House, Inc.

From *Life Expectancy* by Dean Koontz, copyright © 2004 by Dean Koontz, published by Bantam Dell, A Division of Random House, Inc.

From *The Cypress House* by Michael Koryta, copyright © 2011 by Michael Koryta, originally published in hardcover by Little, Brown and Company

From *Brothers in Arms* by Paul Langan and Ben Alirez, copyright © 2004 by Townsend Press, Inc., published by Scholastic, Inc.

From *The Girl with the Dragon Tattoo* by Steig Larsson, translation copyright © 2008 by Reg Keeland, published in the United States by Vintage Books, a division of Random House, Inc.

From *What the Dead Know* by Laura Lippman, copyright © 2007 by Laura Lippman, published by William Morrow, an imprint of HarperCollins Publishers

From *The Devil's Company* by David Liss, copyright © 2009 by David Liss, published in the United States by Random House, an imprint of the Random House Publishing Group, a division of Random House, Inc.

From *I Am Number Four* by Pittacus Lore, copyright © 2010 by Pittacus Lore, published by Harper, HarperCollins Children's Books, a division of HarperCollins Publishers

From *A Feast for Crows* by George R.R. Martin, copyright © 2005 by George R.R. Martin, published in the United States by Bantam Books, an imprint of The Random House Publishing Group, a division of Random House, Inc.

From *A Gate at the Stairs* by Lorrie Moore, copyright

ALSO DISCUSSED

Thirteeen R3asons Why by Jay Asher, copyright © 2007 by Jay Asher, published by Razorbill, Penguin Young Readers Group, the Penguin Group (USA) Inc.

The Lace Reader by Brunonia Barry, copyright © 2006 by Brunonia Barry, published by HarperCollins Publishers

The Maze Runner by James Dashner, copyright © 2009 by James Dashner, published in the United States by Delacorte Press, an imprint of Random House Children's Books, a division of Random House, Inc.

If I Stay by Gayle Forman, copyright © 2009 by Gayle Forman, published by Dutton Books, a member of Penguin Group (USA) Inc.

Into the Woods by Tana French, copyright © 2007 by Tana French, published by the Penguin Group, Penguin Group (USA), Inc.

Never Let Me Go by Kazuo Ishiguro, copyright © 2005 by Kazuo Ishiguro, published by Alfred A. Knopf, a division of Random House, Inc.

Mystic River by Dennis Lehane, copyright © 2001 by Dennis Lehane, published in hardcover by William Morrow, an imprint of Harpercollins Publishers

The Night Circus by Erin Morgenstern, copyright © 2011 by Night Circus, LLC, published in the United States

by Doubleday, a division of Random House, Inc.

Red's Hot Honky-Tonk Bar by Pamela Morsi, copyright © 2009 by Pamela Morsi, published by MIRA Books

Before I Fall by Lauren Oliver, copyright © 2010 by Lauren Oliver, published by HarperCollins Children's Books, a division of HarperCollins Publishers

Treason at Lisson Grove by Anne Perry, copyright © 2011 by Anne Perry, published in the United States by Ballantine Books, an imprint of The Random House Publishing Group, a division of Random House, Inc.

The Virgin of Small Plains by Nancy Pickard, copyright © 2006 by Nancy Pickard, published in the United States by Ballantine Books, an imprint of The Random House Publishing Group, a division of Random House, Inc.

A Field of Darkness by Cornelia Read, copyright © 2006 by Cornelia Read, published by Mysterious Press, Warner Books

The Book Thief by Markus Zusak, copyright © 2005 by Markus Zusak, published in the United States by Alfred A. Knopf, an imprint of Random House Children's Books, a division of Random House, Inc.

CONTENTS

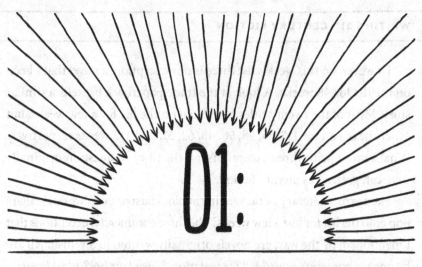

01:

21ST CENTURY FICTION

The *New York Times* Best Sellers List is a rich trove of data, not just for the public, publishers, and booksellers, but also for authors. Many feel that "The List" is meaningless. Literary novelists in particular can see it as a celebration of commercial trash. Commercial writers too may eye it with suspicion, feeling that it's a race rigged by publishers. To be in the running, you had better write thrillers.

Much is changing in our new century. That's true of fiction too, and a close look at the *New York Times* Best Sellers List shows how. As I write (in May 2011), the printed hardcover list has on it fourteen titles which have run for an average of three weeks each.

Think about that. Three weeks? Now, don't get me wrong. Being on the *New York Times* Best Sellers List is never a bad thing. It means that a title is selling at a fast pace. But three weeks on the list doesn't sum up to unit sales on a blockbuster scale. Solid, yes. Enviable, sure. Blockbuster? No.

However, on this week's list there is one exception: a novel that's been on the list for 48 weeks. A look at the trade paperback list tells a similar story. Most of the twenty titles have been on the list for a few weeks, but others have run for 117, 65, 98, 96, 48, 62, 57, and 113 weeks respectively. What's more, with three exceptions, all the titles in question originally were categorized as literary fiction.

Excuse me? Literary fiction selling at blockbuster levels while thrillers pop onto the list for just a few weeks? The three commercial exceptions that I mentioned, by the way, are novels originally written in Swedish. All are by one author who's now dead. Translations? Dead author? *Blockbusters?*

Go back through the list for several years and the picture is the same. *Water for Elephants, The Help, Cutting for Stone, The Art of Racing in the Rain, Hotel on the Corner of Bitter and Sweet, Little Bee, Sarah's Key* ... in our new century, literary fiction is selling the way that commercial novels are supposed to. Certain commercial novelists, on the other hand, are celebrated for their literary quality and simultaneously sell far better than most in their category.

Clearly the 21ˢᵗ century is a counter-intuitive, brain-twisting time for novelists. What's going on? Has public taste changed? Have literary novelists figured something out? Have commercial storytellers somehow slipped up? Is the secret of success a matter of labeling? None of the above.

What's going on is that certain novels are hitting readers with high impact. This impact is both deep and sustained. The word of mouth that it in turn generates is powerful. It wins for these novels readers who are not, empirically, reading other fiction. Commercial fiction is thought to be candy for the masses, but the truth is that the masses are responding in huge numbers to something else entirely.

And what is that? That is the subject of this book. High impact comes from a combination of two factors: great stories and beautiful writing. High-impact novels utilize what is best about literary and commercial fiction. They embrace a dichotomy. They do everything well and as a result sell astoundingly. The publishing industry has a convenient term for these wonder books: *literary/commercial fiction*.

Literary/commercial fiction is the Holy Grail to every editor. To publishers it's black ink. For booksellers it's pure joy. Reading groups embrace these novels, as do librarians, reviewers, teachers, awards committees, and movie producers.

For me, though, literary/commercial fiction is a forecast of where fiction is heading in the 21ˢᵗ century. It's an approach to novel writing that eschews both snobby pretense and genre dogma. It is personal, impassioned, and even downright quirky, yet through its rebellious refusal to please, it paradoxically achieves universal appeal. It panders to no one. It speaks to everyone. My purpose in writing this book is to uncover the secrets of literary/commercial fiction and make its methods a part of every novelist's working practice. Whether your purpose is literary or commercial, regardless if your aim is to enlighten or to entertain, no matter whether you want to give readers what they want or to explore and push boundaries, there are techniques you can take from high-impact fiction to enrich your own.

After all, it's a new century. Everything is changing and fiction is, too. Keeping up is okay, but better still is to zoom ahead of the curve. In these pages I'll show you how to do that.

NEW CENTURY, NEW FICTION

Change is hard. The future is uncertain. That's definitely true in book publishing, where new media is rapidly altering the way that books reach readers and the ways in which authors promote them. Yet strangely, many manuscripts we consider at my literary agency feel stuck in centuries past.

Now, a certain amount of derivative material is to be expected. Trends are eternal, as are their inevitable declines. Gumshoe detectives, Gothic romances, sword and sorcery, sagas, glitz and glitter, supernatural horror, cyberpunk, and many other sub-genres drew in novelists and for a while fed them. The same is happening today with urban fantasy, paranormal romance, and dystopian young adult fiction.

What worries me more are manuscripts that employ the pace, narrative patterns, character types, and even themes of past decades. It's not that flash fiction is the wave of the future, or that we should toss out techniques used by Austen, Dickens, James, Hardy, Verne, Fitzgerald, Hemingway, or Updike to make their novels great. No, but when novels are chained to the past, they cannot speak to the present.

Mechanically mirroring our times isn't automatically better, of course. For instance, shelves today are crowded with protagonists who are haunted, detached, wry, and lost. Heroes and heroines in the classic mold haven't vanished, but in our age readers respond well to wounded daughters and paranormal ops. Consequently, they crowd bookstore shelves. They may reflect our sociological makeup, but they've become clichés.

The characters who resonate most widely today don't merely reflect our times, they reflect ourselves. That's true whether we're talking about genre fare, historicals, satire, or serious literary stuff. Revealing human truths means transcending tropes, peering into the past with fresh eyes, unearthing all that is hidden, and moving beyond what is easy and comfortable to write what is hard and even painful to face.

Get out of the past. Get over trends. To write high-impact 21ˢᵗ century fiction, you must start by becoming highly personal. Find your voice, yes, but more than that, challenge yourself to be unafraid, independent, open, aware, and true to your own heart. You must become your most authentic self.

The journey ahead in this book is a journey into *you*, your strengths and your weaknesses. If you feel discouraged at times, don't freak. Turn to the practical tools that I've provided. They'll show you how to master the methods of high impact.

THE GREAT DIVIDE

As I said, high-impact novels tell great stories and are also beautifully written. Unfortunately, the community of fiction writers is engaged in civil war. That's a shame, since each side has something the other needs.

On one side of the divide are literary novelists, whose bases of operation are MFA programs and literary journals. On the other are commercial storytellers who rally at writers' conferences, train in genre-specific organizations, and bivouac in an online tent city of blogs. The values of these two nations are very different. They seem to despise each other.

Literary novelists create art. They treasure fine writing and seek to capture the world the way it is, making it alive in the minds of their readers. Critical acclaim is their reward; royalties are a rare byproduct and faintly distasteful. Formulas for writing make them suspicious. True art springs organically from within. Novels are honed through a painful process of draft, critique, and revision. Outlines are prisons. Plot is a dirty word. For literary novelists, writing is a lonely pleasure that must be its own reward.

Commercial storytellers want to spin stories that delight readers. Their novels thrill, scare, and stir through a mastery of craft. Strong common values underlie their fiction. Advances, royalties, and best-seller status are measures of success. (Movie deals are nice, too.) Stories that stretch reality are okay if readers buy in. Outlines may not always work for commercial storytellers, but crucial to success are peer support, industry savvy, and self-promotion. Most of all, writing is a joy. Day jobs are for quitting.

Okay, I exaggerate, but you see my point: There are two philosophies of fiction writing. Each champions different intents, processes, and outcomes. Both can produce good fiction, but when adhered to religiously, neither produce novels that reach a vast and diverse audience.

Sadly, the divergence between writing beautifully and spinning great stories is built into our very vocabulary. We speak of "character driven" and "plot driven" novels as if they are mutually exclusive objects. As we'll see, high-impact 21ˢᵗ century fiction is both.

THE PURPOSE OF FICTION

Is fiction a dying art form? It's easy to imagine so, but the truth is that fiction is no more dying than movies or newspapers. The business has changed, sure, but readers still buy certain novels in big numbers.

Not all novels, though. 21ˢᵗ century book consumers support what's important to them. To infuse a novel with a significance that speaks to many requires, paradoxically, that you ignore what the public wants and focus instead on what matters to you. High-impact fiction is highly personal.

E. M. Forster wisely advised, "Only connect!"—but what is it that creates a deep and lasting sense of connection with readers? You would think that story archetypes, everyman characters, and easy-to-read prose would do it. Actually, it's the opposite. High-impact 21ˢᵗ century fiction is built on unique voices, uncommon characters, and tales that can only be told by a particular author. They're *sui generis*.

It's odd, but the universal human experiences that capture our commonality strike us hardest when they're found in unlikely places. Or maybe it's not so strange when you think about it. As a reader, don't you enjoy being swept away into a different world? Do you also love to learn new things? Yet, as much as we crave fresh experience, we also delight in saying, "I totally saw myself in that character," or, "That story was so unusual, but that's exactly the way things are." We search out the familiar in what's exotic.

In other words, if when we least expect it, you surprise us with ourselves, that impact is huge. When a setting is outside our experience yet also feels like our native land, that impact is lasting. When the values underneath your story make us uncomfortable but also somehow sit well with us, that impact is deep. Reaching millions requires reaching into yourself. It means finding your own truth and making it ours.

That, after all, is the purpose of fiction. It explains why fiction remains a vital and popular art form centuries after its creation. It also means that novels will remain a powerful force in the future. High-impact novels define our times and may even change them. Novels have done that in prior centuries and will do so in our century too.

If you have a passion for writing fiction, why not write high-impact 21st century fiction? The result, I believe, can be not just better sales, but fiction that is the fullest expression of what's inside you: stories that hold readers rapt, move their hearts, and even change their minds. Done right, your novels can incite awe in readers.

If that sounds exciting to you, read on. High impact is in your hands.

02:
THE DEATH OF GENRE

RISING ABOVE CATEGORY

They're the envy of their peers. At genre conventions, they deliver the keynotes. Their agents and publishers hover like an entourage. At airport bookstores their latest titles are piled high on tables. Their audio editions are homepage features at online media stores, and their movie deals are significant.

They're the stars: the genre authors whose books sell vastly better than most; so much so that they're no longer labeled genre authors. They're brands. What is it that lifts their indisputably genre novels "out of category"?

Ask readers what they love about great novels and most often they mention great characters. True enough, standout characters are memorable. But if that were all there was to it, the novelist's job would be easy. Needless to say, there's more to it than that.

Deconstruct out-of-category novels and certain common factors emerge: characters we immediately care about, unique worlds, universal human experiences, high tension, plot layers, parallels, reversals, symbols, strong themes. But there's also an X factor: such fiction is personal, meaning that it directly reflects the author's own experience.

When I co-teach workshops with best-selling authors, they are sometimes surprised when I point out how closely their stories parallel their own struggles in life. In working editorially with my writer clients, I often ask, "What in this story makes you angry? What is it that the reader must *get*?" The answers always take us back to the author.

One day I posed those questions to a Grand Master of the Mystery Writers of America. Midway through our work he paused and said, "I just realized why I've been a mid-list writer all my life." It wasn't that his novels didn't reflect his interests and temperament. They did. Yet, while his novels had his stamp, they didn't have his heart—his deepest heart. His stories raised issues but did not plumb his personal pain. The pain he put on the page was generic.

Out-of-category novels use their category conventions merely as a framework. They erect inside them stories that express that which defines not their characters, but their authors. They may have arresting premises, diabolical plots, universal themes, timely issues, or protagonists who tower above the ordinary. All that may be original, but what actually gives fiction its power is that which is personal.

Literary fiction can be as convention-bound as genre fiction. When its tone, voice, characters, and unfolding are dully familiar, then its impact on readers is low. The imagery on the page may feel fresh, but the overall effect is stale. Such fiction strives for originality but instead plays it safe. As with generic commercial fiction, such novels don't so much spring from the soul as serve as a hole in which the author hides.

Whatever type of fiction you intend to write, the greatest challenge you face is to go your own way. Fall back on what is easy and safe and you will stay earthbound. High-impact fiction requires high courage. It means not only doing something different, but delving into what matters to you: what terrifies, outrages, grieves, inspires, hurts, and heals you.

In a day-to-day working sense, going beyond category limitations demands recognizing when you are playing it safe and sidestepping your own traps. It means redirecting your inner compass to point you squarely at whatever makes you afraid.

Out-of-category authors have begun a journey that I wish all novelists would take: a journey away from what is comfortable and convention-bound to fiction that is free, courageous, inventive, and influential because it's utterly unique. It's a place where novelists don't obey genre rules, but summon them when they're useful and bend them to their own purposes.

GENRE BENDING VS. GENRE TRANSCENDING

In the 20th century, genre boundaries were well defined. Not only did readers know which section of a bookstore or library to look for what they liked, they knew what to expect from the novels there. Romance, science fiction, and mysteries all delivered reliable and familiar stories.

The success of strict category storytelling was, in a way, serving its audiences. Housewives and secretaries sought romantic escape. Conservative and older citizens took comfort in stories enacting justice. Scientists, engineers, and computer programmers blasted off to worlds of speculative wonder built with systematic logic. Genres had a sociological appeal.

In the latter part of the 20th century, category lines began to blur. Anne Rice made a hero of a monster. Ellis Peters and Anne Perry set mysteries in the past. Diana Gabaldon wrapped a historical romance inside a time-travel framework. Science and magic could be found in the same novel. Literary fiction borrowed genre elements and even some of its famous characters. All this reflected both a changing demographic among readers and a new breadth of influence among writers. Our world and our fiction grew more complex.

Today, genre bending and blending is more the rule than the exception. Shelves are chock-a-block with literary crime, historical espionage, contemporary urban fantasy, magical women's fiction, dystopian young adult, and paranormal everything.

At my literary agency, when we ponder exciting new novels we'd like to represent, the first question we ask is often, "What category is this?" The issue is not just academic. Although sections have less meaning online and readers browse in ways less linear, the segregation inherent in brick-and-mortar bookstores and publishers' catalogues remains with us.

Individual authors may grow popular enough to transcend category and become front-of-store brands, but new novelists cannot escape a choice of launching pads. The choice can be confounding. A frequent question I get in pitch sessions at writers' conferences is, "What category am I?" When I respond with the question, "Where do you think your readers will look for you in a physical bookstore?" the answer is often a shrug. "I just write the stuff."

While that answer can be a cop-out, it may also express a genuine indifference to traditional category borders. To be sure, there are genre purists. Mention Margaret Atwood's *The Handmaid's Tale* (1985) to a hard-core science-fiction writer and you're likely to get a rant. Even the new sub-categories have produced new orthodoxies and narrow award categories to celebrate them. Just look at the RITA and Golden Heart award categories of the Romance Writers of America. *Best Paranormal Romance?* Talk about specific!

In a way it's good for genre-specific fiction to get support. The need of genre authors for recognition, respect, advocacy, education, and networking shows in the growing number of such organizations. Mystery Writers of America was founded in 1945, Science Fiction Writers of America in 1965, Romance Writers of America in 1981, Horror Writers Association in 1986 and International Thriller Writers in 2004. Fantasy writers are long overdue for a splinter group. Who knows? Maybe we'll see steampunk or paranormal writers band together to advance their interests.

It's natural for people to group together along common lines. The same is true for writers. Yet, while this tendency is understandable, it also can work against what gives fiction high impact. A genre-blending novel may be original, true, but that does not automatically make it personal and powerful fiction.

When a hot trend turns into a sub-category, new strictures arise along with it. Tropes turn into shortcuts, character paradigms become cardboard cutouts. Publishing pulls the bandwagon, true enough, but when feel-alike fiction floods the market its impact declines because it is starved of what makes fiction rich, surprising, moving, and masterful.

To put it differently, blending genres doesn't bust a novelist free of genre boundaries. It can simply put one in a new box.

So, whether you are a genre stalwart or a barrier breaker, what is it that will lift your fiction to brand-level sales? Look at highly successful novelists who've started sub-categories, like Anne Perry with historical mysteries, Diana Gabaldon with time-travel romance, Jim Butcher with urban fantasy. Each blended genres, sure, but each has also won vast audiences while their imitators have fallen away. Why? They are first of all effective novelists. Their stories may be commercial in profile, but their skill and personal passion turn into stories of high impact.

I'm no genre purist. My literary agency has prospered thanks to genre-blending fiction. We often are glad that we took on novelists who were initially hard to classify. Their groundbreaking ideas can be harder to launch, but once airborne can fly high. Out-of-the-box story ideas hit readers with their novelty, no doubt, but there's another reason why such authors are successful.

Perhaps in part because they have fewer rules to follow, they must rely more on universal techniques and stay truer to their inner compasses. Without genre crutches to lean on they must walk the walk of true novelists. You can call them genre-bending if you like, but I call them genre-transcending. While they may establish a new category, they are genuine fiction masters.

GENRE FICTION OR LITERATURE?

A curious phenomenon has arisen in recent years. It's the appearance of genre fiction so well written that it attains a status and recognition usually reserved for literary works.

Sometimes, in fact, it's hard to tell what the author's intention truly was. Is Alan Furst foremost a writer of espionage? When Robert Stone wrote *Damascus Gate* (1999), did he intend to write a thriller? Michael Chabon combined both a speculative premise and a murder mystery in *The Yiddish Policeman's Union* (2007), yet his novel is more than the sum of those parts.

That blurriness is even more noticeable in the realm of women's fiction. If there's a dividing line between serious and entertaining, on which side of it is Kristin Hannah? Barbara Delinsky? Caroline Leavitt? Are Iain Banks, Jonathan Lethem, and Neal Stephenson science-fiction writers or something else?

At genre conventions the debate over genre boundaries is almost a sport. Only two conclusions seem to me certain: Genre writers don't get enough respect, and when they do they don't get much respect from genre writers. It's as if the only worthy credentials are being born in the ghetto and hanging out there still. Literary types can be just as snobby. *It's true that I made Arthur Conan Doyle a character, but* (shudder) *don't label me a mystery writer, puh-lease!*

For me, where genre ends and literature begins doesn't matter. What matters is whether a given novel hits me with high impact. If it does, it probably is fulfilling the purpose of fiction. It has drawn me into a story world, held me captive, taken me on a journey with characters like none I've ever met, revealed truths I've somehow always known and insights that rock my brain. It's filled me with awe, which is to say it's made me see the familiar in a wholly new way and made the unfamiliar a foundational part of me. It both entertains and matters. It both captures our age and becomes timelessly great. It does all that with the sturdy tools of story and the flair of narrative art.

If you've ever finished reading a novel, set it down, and felt like you were walking in a dream rather than walking to the kitchen sink to wash out your tea mug, then you've felt the impact I'm talking about. It's more than being swept away, entertained, surprised, and satisfied. It's being engaged on emotional levels new to you, and challenged in ways that make you glad. It's taking a journey unlike any other and finding it's your own. It's waking to a world completely different and finding that it's as familiar as the rhythm of your heart.

Powerful story and beautiful writing bound together may confound critics and fill fellow writers with envy, but it will surely reach readers. Who cares if you can't be classified? The imaginations that matter are those glued to your pages. It's readers for whom you're writing and no one else.

PUSHED TO THE FRINGE?

Blazing trails and writing from highly personal places bring with them natural worries: *What if I'm ahead of the curve? What if my subject matter is too strange or my approach too unconventional? What if no one wants to hear what I'm saying?*

Do your subject matter or character choices doom you to fringe status? Hmm, let's think. Is slavery a non-commercial topic? Sorry about that, Harriet Beecher Stowe, Alex Haley, and David Fuller. Are gay protagonists going to limit your audience? Christopher Isherwood and Armistead Maupin, better try again!

Are there narrative strategies that are automatic turn-offs? Do tales told in reverse confuse readers? If so, maybe Philip K. Dick and Martin Amis should have come up with different ideas for *Counter-Clock World* (1967) and *Time's Arrow* (1991). Is time travel a minor-league science fiction gimmick? Someone should have mentioned that to Mark Twain before he wrote *A Connecticut Yankee in King Arthur's Court* (1889) or Stephen King before he thought up *11/22/63* (2011).

Do unpopular points or morally challenging themes mean that you're going to be marginalized? Oh, dear. That would be bad news for Anthony Trollope, Philip Pullman, and Jodi Picoult. Are emotional extremes bad for sales? Maybe Sylvia Plath should have trashed *The Bell Jar* (1963), and James Lee Burke should have shelved *Last Car to Elysian Fields* (2003).

As you can see, when writing fiction with high impact, there's no subject matter too taboo, no character too eccentric, no emotional content too intense, no themes too difficult. It's all in how you handle it. What overcomes all objections are characters who compel, stories that grip, and writing that amazes.

It's true that some manuscripts cause publishers to scratch their heads and pass. *I love this but I don't know how to publish it* is a common, if frustrating, example from rejection e-mails. That kind of response tells me that much is going right with the novel, but not enough. Dark fiction may have protagonists who are hard to care about. Satire may lack enough bite. Cross-genre fiction may not be forging a new alloy, but rather be torn between two equally enjoyable but clashing intentions.

The solution in such cases is not to play it safe but instead to find the strongest possible way to play a risky gambit. If protagonists are made compelling, then readers will follow them to hard places. Unfamiliar story patterns work when their hidden chronology is carefully prepared. Challenging moral points will sway when they're grounded in what's good.

Instead of worrying about what's fringe, focus on what gives fiction high impact. Weak writing can sink traditionally popular story types. By contrast, skillful story technique can sell even the most outrageous premises and protagonists. Check out Vladimir Nabokov's *Lolita* (1955) and Yann Martel's *Life of Pi* (2001). They turned fringe into famous. You can, too.

THE DEATH OF GENRE

If there were a manifesto for 21st century fiction writers, I hope it would go like this: *Down with high-flown literature! Cast off genre servitude!* The revolution is founded in authorial liberty. It regards story and art as equals.

Don't get me wrong. I hope that in a hundred years we'll still be reading novels about love, murder, and saving the world. I hope the adventure, healing, and coming-of-age novel will never go out of style. Fiction that illuminates human experience will also always be welcomed by me. What I do hope will perish, though, are novels that imitate, cash in on trends, lean on familiar formulas, and follow the safe road to validation. Readers agree. They're taking their stand at retail cash registers and by hitting the "Purchase" button on their touch screens.

The term *genre* has a pejorative ring, yet there is also nothing automatically superior about literary fiction. I encourage all novelists to ignore status games, get over envy, and remember what makes us write fiction in the first place: the desire to tell the stories in our hearts, capture all that makes our existence grand, rattle readers' presumptions, affirm our common values, shine a light on our age, and spin tales both utterly unique and universally loved.

You can do that from any starting point. Find a framework you like, or simply choose something you wish to say. There's no single methodology for high-impact storytelling. What matters is mastery of narrative skills and skillful use of the finest methods of the storyteller's art.

The death of genre will come for you on the day that you cut yourself loose from your fears. When you stop writing like you think you are supposed to and start writing in the way that only you can, then you will discover the impact you can have.

You'll know you've achieved that when no one any longer slots you in a category and you've become a category by yourself. Sure, let the industry label you a brand. I'm fine with that. But on the day that genre finally and truly dies for you, you'll become what you're meant to be: a true novelist.

⟐ 21ˢᵀ CENTURY TOOLS ⟐

TRANSCENDING GENRE CONVENTIONS

- What's your favorite kind of fiction? What's your favorite thing about it? Narrow that to a single element or event. Find and heighten that in your own manuscript. Celebrate it. Delight in it.
- Now take that heightened element or event and reverse it. A novel that does the opposite would do what? Do that.
- Now take that element or event and eliminate it altogether. Do you really need it?
- What does your favorite kind of fiction get wrong? How does it cheat, lie, or slide by? What's it missing? Correct that defect in your manuscript.
- What's an iron rule of your genre? What do fans demand? Break that rule. Deny that expectation. How can you do so more deliberately?
- Write down three overused words in your type of story. Search your manuscript for those words. Uh-oh.

WRITING PERSONALLY

- Stop. Think. What's on your mind today? What question preoccupies you? What's the most recent lesson you've learned? Find a spot to give those thoughts to a character.
- Your computer has crashed. Your backup has failed. Your printouts have burned. Write out in one paragraph why your novel matters. In which character's mouth do those words belong?
- Use that paragraph in another way: What event in your novel best demonstrates what you've written? That's your moral climax. Revise that scene, strip away excess, until its meaning is diamond-hard.

- When was the last time you cried? What's one physical object, sound, or other sensory detail you remember from that moment? Find a spot where your protagonist cries. Add that detail.
- Why did you cry? Anyone would cry over that, but for you what was especially hurtful? Does your protagonist cry over the same thing? Why not? Make it happen.
- What's your greatest joy? The mystery you can't solve? The flaw you can't fix? The most important thing in your life? Give any (or all) of that to your protagonist.
- What's your favorite song? How does it transport you? (Be specific.) Find a spot to transport your protagonist in the same way.
- What's your favorite food? Beyond its flavor, what does devouring that food represent for you? Find a spot to nourish your protagonist in exactly that way.
- What will you do anything to avoid? What for you is its sharpest edge? Cut your protagonist with it.
- What do you wish you were that you're not? Who in your novel can become your fantasy self? Presto.

GENRE TRANSCENDING

- In twenty minutes, write out a parody of your genre, sub-genre, or story type. Be wicked. Then take a look. What in your parody is uncomfortably close to your own manuscript? Oops.
- Is your novel more than one kind of thing? A romance wrapped inside a mystery in an historical setting? (Or anything blended?) No problem. Take each story element and outline it, as if that were the entire novel. Work until it could be an entire novel.
- Two genres or story intentions co-exist in your novel? Okay. Each says the same thing in a different way . . . what is it? Work until the parallel feels (to you) ridiculously obvious.

- What's the universal message in your type of story? You believe that, too, but would spin it a little differently. Write down that spin. Where in the story, and how, will you make that clear?
- Suppose you're actually living in your story. Who are you? If you're in the story already, make that character more like the real you in one way. (If you're not in the story already, come on, get in there.)

STORY + QUALITY

- In your opinion, what's the most artful trick of great novelists? Work that trick in your manuscript. Now it's yours, too.
- What's a moment in your story that sparkles in your mind? Spend an hour with it. Polish. Buff. Shine.
- What's a nasty truth about people that nobody wants to hear? Dramatize that strongly once in your manuscript.
- What in your experience is truly wonderful about human beings? Create a story moment that enacts that.
- Pick a favorite novel by someone else. What about it is enormous fun? Have the same fun in yours.
- What's your novel going to say that fans of your story type definitely won't like? Say it louder.
- Make sure of the following: 1) In the world of your story there's something no one has ever seen before; 2) There's something everyone will recognize.

03:

THE INNER JOURNEY

EMOTIONAL LANDSCAPE

A story's action generates in readers excitement and interest. Conflict—especially micro-tension (which we'll explore in greater detail in chapter six)—keeps readers involved. Associative devices like metaphor, simile, symbols, parallels, reversals, and references contribute a sense of meaning. Meaning itself in the form of theme is necessary for high impact.

But what is it that moves readers' hearts? What conjures in readers' imaginations a reality that, for a while, feels more real than their own lives? What glues readers to characters and makes those characters objects of identification: people with whom readers feel intimately involved, about whom they care, and whose outcomes matter greatly?

Emotions. When readers feel little or nothing, then a story is just a collection of words. It's empty. To foster reader involvement, it is first critical to map an emotional landscape across which readers will travel. Readers must feel that they are on a journey, one with felt significance and a destination that we can sum up as change.

In some literary circles there is a suspicion that emotions on the page are bad. This Hemingway-like way of looking at it values imagery, restraint, subtext, and suggestiveness. Raw emotions written out on the page are viewed as artless. Emotions evoked are artful, particularly when a given emotion has no name but nevertheless feels covertly real. You don't need to name it. Indeed, don't. But make your readers experience something "true," as in accurate.

Look, there's nothing wrong with restraint. Working with subtext is artful. Familiar emotions, especially when in neon lights, have little effect on readers. By contrast, going sideways to explore secondary and nuanced emotions can bring a fictional moment ferociously alive. I'm not against artfulness. I'm for it because it works. But eschewing emotions as a style, in the false belief that a drought somehow quenches thirst, is too often an excuse for a novelist to hide. Sere writing can be as mannered and false, in its way, as the most purple genre fare.

To create a novel's emotional landscape you must first open yourself to your own. That's hard to do. If it's difficult to confide your feelings to those close to you, consider how much more fearful it is to do that with strangers. But that's what you're doing. Whether you're aware of it or not, there is wired inside you a terror of exposing yourself to embarrassment, shame, and ridicule. But here you are writing fiction. Are you nuts? Or, more to the point, is that what people will think of you when they read your work?

The inhibiting effect of shame cannot be overstated. It explains why some writers slide into genre clichés or literary imitation. To put authentic emotions on the page, you need to own them. When you do, readers will respect you. It's when you hide that readers feel shortchanged, cheated, and only minimally involved.

Set down the emotions that you believe you should use and it's pretty much a guarantee that a given passage will feel glib. On the other hand, if you capture emotions that are fresh, genuine, specific to your character, and unique to the situation, then you will overrun readers' defenses. You'll take them by surprise. Readers feel resistance, too. They fear high feelings as much as you do. Paradoxically, it's also what they seek in fiction. If you have ever raged or cried when reading a novel and cursed the author for making you feel like that, then you've experienced that resistance.

Recognize that, above all things, you likely were hurt in childhood. Unless you've had a lot of psychotherapy, those hurts are with you still. If they hurt enough, you might unconsciously re-create the old painful circumstances in your current relationships. I mention this because it's helpful to the fiction process. Your deepest hurts are a wellspring of passion. Projecting old conflicts onto current relationships probably doesn't work, but projecting it into your stories does. Don't fight it. Many novelists aren't even aware that they're doing it. But when there's passion on the page, it probably flows from buried rage, the sting of injustice, unhealed trauma, or the ache for love.

Deep stuff. Painful feelings. Beautiful material! One of the joys of writing 21ˢᵗ century fiction is the permission it gives you to feel deeply and wide. Your task is to tune yourself to the frequency where honest emotions come through with a crackle and hiss. It can be hard to find them amid the blast of the powerful-but-familiar emotional playlists crowding the dial.

Fortunately, there are tools and techniques to help you sift out what's authentic. Emotions that come in primary colors like anger, fear, desire, resolve, and envy are fine, but hammer readers dully because they're familiar. Anything described as "gut-twisting" isn't going to twist readers' guts. Secondary emotions can bring subtlety and nuance to a scene. Sometimes it's also useful to reverse yourself and force onto the page an emotion that's the opposite of what you first thought to write down.

Better still are emotions that surprise. Best of all are emotions that conflict. The prompts at the end of this chapter can help you find them. Work toward building an instinct for emotional originality. When you've got that, you'll be painting emotional landscapes that are constantly intriguing and even provocative for travelers.

The more sudden are the turns, the steeper the climbs, and the most astounding the vistas, the more readers will connect to the landscape. The trip you take them on is one they'll take inside. It will feel like a memory, even though you invented it at the keyboard.

INNER CONFLICT AND DOWNWARD DESCENT

Once you are in the habit of writing with authentic emotion, the next step is to get comfortable with conflicting feelings. Conflicting feelings snare readers. They're a puzzle that demands solution, a cognitive dissonance that's too noisy to ignore. Conflicting feelings that persist, escalate, and cannot easily be resolved can become inner conflict, which is one of the greatest ways to create fascinating and memorable characters.

Inner conflict is an interior war. Like an invasion unfolding live on television, it's a gripping contest that keeps readers glued. While conflicting feelings are a momentary effect, inner conflict can echo in readers' minds years after they finish a novel.

The strongest inner conflicts plague characters with two desires that are mutually exclusive. When believably built, inner conflict leads to unsettling actions. It tests, torments, and defines. It becomes utterly necessary. It becomes part of the plot.

Please don't confuse inner conflict with inner turmoil, a messy indecision, waffling, and weakness that turns readers off. Inner conflict is a dilemma. It's a debate that can't be won, an unavoidable fork in a road that leads to two equally feared or desired destinations. It's a predicament that's powerfully human.

The snappy heroine of Joshilyn Jackson's literary crime hybrid success *gods in Alabama* (2005) has conflict poured into her foundation. As a graduate student in Chicago, Arlene Fleet has sworn to God (big "G" this time) three things: 1) She will stop screwing every boy who crosses her path; 2) She will never again tell a lie, not even a small one; 3) She will never return to her family and hometown of Possett, Alabama. Arlene has good reasons for this. Before leaving Possett she had sex with fifty-two of the fifty-three boys in her sophomore class, in order of their sixteenth birthdays, and lived a whopping great lie. Fact is that ten years earlier Arlene murdered a boy, Jim Beverly, her high school's golden boy and football hero, whose body was never found.

Having given Arlene good reasons not to return to Possett, however, Jackson then makes it imperative for her heroine to go back. The reasons are both internal and external. Internally, Arlene is carrying a crushing load of guilt. Her family also is pressuring her to visit home. Her boyfriend, Burr, is frustrated with her refusal to sleep with him. Her scrupulous truth telling is twisting her in knots. And then there's the external reason: On her doorstep arrives an unwelcome visitor, Rose Mae Lolley, the only witness on the night that Arlene murdered Jim Beverly and who, like most of Possett, believes he's still alive. Rose was in love with him and now wants to find him. Exposure looming, Arlene must return to Possett to cover her backside.

Although Arlene's decision to return to Possett is made early in the novel, the push-pull inner conflict that Jackson has constructed for her infuses the remainder of the story. Arlene doesn't want the truth to come out, yet she needs the truth to come out. And it does. In case you were worried, Arlene killed Jim Beverly for good reasons—reasons which also explain her promiscuity. It's also not clear that he's really dead. Jackson cleverly builds Arlene's inner conflict through the middle of the novel by also making Jim Beverly's villainy somewhat ambiguous:

> I couldn't help but be glad the rapist was dead. I had a secret fierce joy that I'd erased him from the earth, and I felt the earth was better with one less rapist on it. But I had also killed someone's son. His father's picture in the paper, worried and earnest, haunted

me. I had killed the boy who'd fought for Rose Mae Lolley, and at school she wafted through the halls, tiny and lost with black circles under her luminous eyes. The rapist and the boy who gave me his jacket to cover the blood on my pants and made me laugh my way out of shame were the same boy.

Inner conflict works powerfully when it's big and unavoidable, and when it builds as a story goes on. Joshilyn Jackson does this to great effect in *gods in Alabama*. What about you? How is your main character inwardly conflicted? How can he be more so? How can that conflict box her in? How can it escalate to a point impossible to endure? Make that happen and your main characters will wage inside them internal wars that are difficult for your readers to escape.

Another way to create dynamism in the inner life of a character is to turn a flaw or shortcoming into a struggle: a struggle that involves defeats, costs, crisis, and finally change. Think of it as a mini-arc. Not all character growth is an upward curve. Sometimes it's a downward descent into our darker selves.

You've probably never heard of Bluford High in Southern California. People don't want to know about the Bluford Highs of this world. It's a school whose population is largely black. It's poor. Families struggle. Kids have problems. But the series of short, street tough, tell-it-like-it-is Bluford High novels have found a huge readership among those very kids. The stories are stark morality tales, packed with inescapable traps and life-changing choices. They're simple, gut-wrenching, violent, and real.

Brothers in Arms (2004) by Paul Langan and Ben Alirez tells the story of sixteen-year-old Marty Luna, whose eight-year-old brother Huero is killed while trying to protect Marty during a drive-by shooting. Shortly afterward, Marty's mother moves them to a different part of town. Marty goes to Bluford High, but has trouble as we find out immediately in the framework opening as Marty faces the displeasure of Principal Spencer:

"What's the problem between you and Steve Morris?" she asked.

"Nothin'," I said. Even though I hate the kid, I ain't a rat.

She crossed her arms and sighed, still looking at me as if I was some kind of a puzzle. I could see she was losing patience. I don't blame her. I ain't easy to deal with. Still, I stared back at her until she was forced to look away. You can't stare me down. I've been hit by people who would scare you on the street. I don't run from anyone, not principals or kids like Steve Morris who give me trouble. That's part of my problem.

Marty's inner struggle, naturally enough, is to resist using violence. With his buried guilt, grief, and rage over his brother's murder, as well as his relocation to a new school, this struggle is difficult. Marty is taunted by the Bluford blowhard, star jock Steve Morris. More dangerously, his old neighborhood gang has sworn to avenge Huero's death and they eventually do discover who's responsible. The good angels on Marty's other shoulder are his mother, a caring English teacher, and a pretty girl named Vicky, who sees through Marty's tough exterior.

For most of the novel, Marty loses his inner struggle. He can't help it. Even getting an "A" on an English essay on the subject of heroes (his hero is his dead brother) isn't enough encouragement. Vicky's budding love isn't strong enough. Marty must make the worst mistakes. He fights. He's expelled. Finally he goes for a vengeance ride with his old gang, heading for the certain loss of everything he could have. Only at the last minute does he remember something his little brother said, and then he changes:

> Truth is, we'd only be creating another mess. Another broken family. Another crying mother. Another plot to collect tears in the graveyard. Another headstone in a growing sea of graves.
>
> Not me. Not Martin Luna. Not anymore.
>
> "There's just too many dead people," Huero had said. My little brother was right. He taught me. There had to be another way. I thought of one. Even if it was a long shot. I had to try it.

> I opened the car door.
>
> "Whatcha doin', Martin?" Chago asked.
>
> "Leaving." I stepped out and started walking to Bluford.

Stark. Simple. Effective. But it's effective only because Marty descended so far in the wrong direction. To lift a character high, they must sink low. It's scary, I know, but the change makes it worthwhile.

Inner conflict and downward descents are strong ways to bring the inner life of a character alive, but many authors mistakenly believe they're all that's necessary to give a novel emotional grip. Not true. For an inner journey to fully engross readers, it needs to be thoroughgoing. As human beings we're not just about our quandaries and bad habits. Our inner lives are deep and multifold.

GOING HOME, SECRETS, SHAME, AND REGRET

Beyond our characters' immediate preoccupations lie their needs for healing, happiness, wholeness, and self-understanding. The inner journey is just beginning. Its next level takes us toward that which has shaped our characters and keeps them from becoming what they desire to be. It's a painful journey home to heal.

It's no accident that the journey toward wholeness often involves an actual return to a character's childhood home. The place where one grew up is the setting for all that shaped, hurt, and propelled him down the paths taken in adulthood. Going forward happily isn't possible until one has first traveled backward to reconcile with the past.

Does that sound like psychotherapy? Perhaps it is, but it's also a fundamental human need. It explains why this part of the journey constantly recurs in successful fiction. The healing journey resonates with readers. It's a staple element in women's fiction, but it also can deepen and add impact to other types of stories.

Contemporary crime fiction (or is it literary fiction?) is chock-a-block with examples of returning to the past, if not to one's actual hometown, to find resolution. Joshilyn Jackson's *gods in Alabama* (mentioned earlier) is one example. So is Cornelia Read's *A Field of Darkness* (2006), in which Madeline Dare, a rebellious daughter of old money, learns that her blue-blood family is connected to a twenty-year-old double murder, and revisits them to learn the truth of things and make peace with her past. Brunonia Barry's *The Lace Reader* (2006) also involves a return home, this time to spooky Salem, Massachusetts, where Barry's unstable heroine, Towner Whitney, reencounters her family of fortune-telling "lace readers," as well as secrets involving a dead baby, a cult, witchcraft, the Underground Railroad, and the disappearance of her aunt and another local woman.

There's more. Tana French's *In the Woods* (2007) brings a Dublin police detective back to the scene of a horror from his childhood, a woods where he and two other children were found in blood-soaked socks and shoes with no memory of what happened. Nancy Pickard's *The Virgin of Small Plains* (2006) sends not one but three adults backward to uncover the truth of the night seventeen years earlier when a naked teenage runaway (whose grave later becomes an object of veneration) was found dead in the snow near their small Kansas town, her face battered beyond recognition, an event that changed the course of each of their lives.

And then there's the granddaddy of all haunted-by-the-past crime novels, Dennis Lehane's *Mystic River* (2001), which also sends three former friends—now a crook, a CPA, and a detective—on a journey to discover the truth of what happened when, as boys, one of them was abducted. He survived; but what happened during the days he was missing? When the daughter of the crook disappears, the CPA (the abducted one) comes home covered in blood, and the detective is assigned to the case. This rich stew of suspicion, survivor guilt, and personal struggles builds to a climax of Greek tragedy proportions. As you can see, the past is a perilous minefield and a powerful narrative tool, but only if you make it so.

In constructing mysteries to plant in the past, the trick is to use misdirection to keep the truth from being obvious; also, to make the revelations, when they arrive, big if not shocking. Just as useful to story construction is the heavy emotional baggage that goes with kept secrets: that is, shame. Shame is a powerful motivator. When used weakly, though, it motivates only avoidance, delay, and inertia. When used well, it generates action.

Jenna Blum's *The Stormchasers* (2010) revolves around Karena Jorge, a writer for the *Minneapolis Ledger*. On her thirty-eighth birthday, Karena learns that her bipolar twin brother, Charles, whom she has not seen in twenty years, has briefly checked into and been released from a clinic in Wichita, Kansas. Karena interprets this as a sign that her brother needs her. To find him, she signs up for a tornado tour, knowing that if she's going to find Charles anywhere, it will be in pursuit of the twisters with which he's obsessed.

What would motivate a successful journalist to chuck her job and chase tornadoes in pursuit of a brother who has hidden himself for twenty years? The bond between twins is powerful, of course, and is nicely built in the novel's middle back–story section. But is that enough? Really, Karena could hire a detective to find Charles. There has to be more, and there is: a secret the two have kept for twenty years. It weighs on Karena and that weight must be lifted. Or, to put it another way, she can no longer bear the shame. When Charles signals "find me," Karena goes . . . and comes harrowingly close to the real tornados that are as chaotic and violent as her brother's manic episodes.

Indeed, it's such a manic episode that comprises the secret. Flashback to their eighteenth birthday (a parallel—see chapter seven), and Charles's mania is beginning to manifest. He drives the two of them into the blinding heart of a tornado—and kills a motorcycle rider. That's a tragic event, but by itself it is not enormously shocking (would you agree?). Shame sets in when Karena agrees not to tell. Since they're now eighteen, Charles can be prosecuted as an adult. Neglected in prison, overlooked, and bipolar, he'll be lost forever. So she keeps quiet. But that's not the only source of her shame. Shortly afterward, she reports a suicide attempt by Charlie. As he is taken away, betrayed and terrified, he extracts a promise from Karena that she will come for him.

But she doesn't. Before leaving for university she takes a drive with her best friend Tiff and breaks down crying, and a shame strong enough to overshadow the subsequent twenty years sets in:

> The Mississippi flows slowly by and the sun shines clean over everything, and Karena knows Tiff thinks she is crying because of Charles, because her brother is stuck in a mental asylum instead of out and about on this beautiful day the way he should be, healthy and alert and comfortable in his own skin. And this is true; she is. But even more Karena is crying for herself. She cries because of her cowardice, because she told Charles she would come back and never did. She cries because of her selfishness, because she has turned him in not just so he could get help but so she would be free to go. She cries because of these things she has discovered in her own cold heart, and most of all she cries because there are so many things she will never be able to tell anyone, not even her best friend; because her whole life long, there will be so much nobody will ever know.

Twenty years later, the shame and guilt she's carried propels Karena into action; indeed, it propels her into the dark heart of tornados—and the past. It takes a powerful secret, and a mountain of shame, to make such a course of action convincing.

Have you ever faced your own cold heart? Not nice, is it? What about your characters? What secrets are they keeping? What is causing them shame? Build those powerfully and they will powerfully propel your story.

The journey to one's past isn't limited to protagonists. Antagonists and secondary characters of course have histories, too. Touching on the past of any character instantly adds depth and dimension.

If you find this phase of the inner journey uncomfortable, you might take a look at why. Do you find a protagonist's self-examination weak, wallowing, and a distraction from the forward momentum of the plot? I understand, but remember that a story's impact depends on its emotional grip on the reader. Plot means excitement, but it's what happens externally. It's the internal life of a character that connects to the reader's heart, and the most intense slice of that is the part that's the most personal: the past.

CUSTOMIZING THE INNER JOURNEY

Does a journey home to heal sound to you gooey, phony, and cheap? No problem. There are as many ways to plumb depths of character as there are characters to plumb. Indeed, the most satisfying inner journeys are the ones you custom make for your characters.

Constructing an inner journey for any character starts with discovering where that character would least like to go. What's the hardest truth to accept? What's the most fearful experience and why? Who has earned your main character's undying hatred or unwarranted respect? What has he sworn never to do? What does she hope for the hardest? What principle is too solid to stand up in a storm? What destination is too distant ever to be reached?

Anything dear and important is an Achilles' heel. It's the chink in the armor for which to aim. Drive in an axe and open it up. Underneath anything fundamental is a fear. A source of strength always conceals a weakness. What matters will surely be tested, and through that testing you'll find everything your character needs in order to learn what she is made of. After that, it's a matter of making that education require as many steps as possible.

Many authors talk about putting their characters through a wringer. That's a good metaphor, but prolong the squeeze. Work backwards from the final realization to identify every reason for resistance, all the possible help that can fail, every reason to cling to the old self and, ultimately, the source of greatest fear.

With that task list in hand, find a way to turn everything you've listed into an event. An inner moment can work, but observable action is better.

For every step in the journey, ask, "What can my character do here?" Better still, "What's the biggest and most dramatic thing she can do?" Best of all, "What don't I want my character to do?" Ah. That could be even better on the page.

Jamie Ford's massively successful debut novel, *Hotel on the Corner of Bitter and Sweet* (2009), is the story of Henry Lee, who as a Chinese-American boy in Seattle during World War II falls in love with a Japanese-American girl, Keiko Okabe. They are separated when she and her family are interred in one of America's most shameful wartime hypocrisies.

Henry's inner journey involves a reconciliation of his American and Chinese heritages (the latter represented by his Chinese Nationalist father). This reconciliation is kicked off in 1986 when the Panama Hotel, once the gateway to Seattle's Japantown, undergoes a renovation. Discovered in the basement are the sad belongings left behind by Japanese families arrested during the war. Among these artifacts are Keiko's sketchbooks, including a portrait of young Henry.

Henry's memories of the events of the early 1940s are his journey. Meeting Keiko working in a school cafeteria, their shared love of local jazz, and his pursuit of her all the way to an internment facility called Camp Harmony—all this brings Henry up against the contradictory, impossible-to-reconcile forces in his life. Keiko disappears; Henry, who wears a protective button stating "I am Chinese," lives through the war and eventually marries a local girl, Ethel, with whom he has a son and a happy life.

Yet something is missing for Henry. He has a lost love. How can he make peace with that, even though his life was, in essence, content? Threaded through the novel (more on this in chapter six) is Henry's uneasy relationship with his son, Marty, who is engaged to a Caucasian girl, Samantha. She wins over her future father-in-law by cooking an extraordinary Chinese dinner, and Henry finally makes peace with his own Chinese heritage and the loss of Keiko:

Henry had thought about Keiko off and on through the years— from a longing, to a quiet, somber acceptance, to sincerely wishing her the best, that she might be happy. That was when he realized that he did love her. More than what he'd felt all those years ago. He loved her enough to let her go—to not go dredging up the past. And besides, he had Ethel, who had been a loving wife. And of course, he had loved her as well. And when she fell ill, he would have changed places with her if he could. To see her get up and walk again, he'd gladly have lain down in that hospice bed. But in the end, he was the one who had to keep living.

The inner journey in Ford's novel is hardly a generic transformation. It's the arrival of inner peace for a Chinese-American resident of Seattle, whose story is so close to and yet so tragically different from that of the Japanese-American girl he once loved and never forgot. It's a highly specific journey. Yet strangely, isn't Henry's journey the same as everyone's? Who doesn't have a lost love? Who doesn't have a regret which must be let go?

Remember, too, that an inner journey isn't a lone excursion. Whether we want it or not, our struggles are shared by family and friends. The effects of our changes ripple outward to the pond at large.

CHANGE AND SERIES CHARACTERS

Series fiction is popular, and it's easy to see why. Returning book after book to beloved characters and places is comforting. Lingering problems and personal issues act like cliffhangers. Readers are nosy neighbors who always want to see what's going on.

Writers of series fiction, naturally enough, tend to hold things back. An arc or back-story revelation for a secondary character is saved for the next book because, hey, there's another manuscript under contract that's got to be filled somehow. The biggest way in which I notice this hoarding is with respect to protagonists' inner conflicts. Bring a main character up against something huge and transformative and, well, you've blown that wad. What's left for future books? As more than one writer has said to me, "How many times can I put my guy through the wringer?"

Long-running series can run into the simple problem of exhaustion. Historical novelist Anne Perry ran into that situation after twenty-five books in her long-running Victorian series featuring humbly-born Inspector Thomas Pitt and his high-born wife Charlotte. During a story conference she confided to me that she didn't know what more she could do with Pitt. "Has he ever killed someone?" I asked. He hadn't. I then posed the question, "What else has he never had to do, and how could it be what he fears most?"

Perry's answer was to promote Pitt from inspector in Special Branch, the police department assigned to cases of high political sensitivity, to commander. No longer responsible for just following orders, Pitt now has to decide in the first place which cases are to become active, knowing that the mere fact of opening an investigation itself ruins lives and reputations. In the twenty-sixth book in the series, *Treason at Lisson Grove* (2011), Pitt not only faces this burden but at the end, with knowledge of guilt but insufficient evidence to prove it, faces a ruthless traitor alone with gun in hand. He must decide whether to shoot the man dead.

Once again, Perry puts Pitt through the wringer. There is always a new way to test, gut, and even transform a long-running series character. That's because there's always something new challenging us in life. Are the issues you face now the same as a decade ago? What new worries kept you awake last night? What is currently testing your patience, your principles, or your beliefs? What's the worst thing that could happen to you today? How exactly are you unready for that? What's making you angry? What questions remain unanswered? What are you avoiding? In what way could you improve? What's blocking you from being a better person?

Any of those questions can be thrown at your series protagonist. The answer will be an opening to what your character fears, avoids, and worries about. It's a window to what remains unresolved. After that, you need only create a story that unavoidably brings your character up against those things.

Test, torment, and transform.

Easy, right?

Managing the payout in a series is tricky. Most series authors have ending points planned: ultimate showdowns and final revelations. That's good. But when a series saves up too much and starts to coast, falling into a pattern or imitating itself, readers begin to feel bored. The results are royalty statements that plateau or even decline.

The antidote is not to bring on the big finale sooner than planned but to fill each volume with emotional importance for your protagonist. Why make it easy? For once in life, it's best not to save. Find a new way to put your series characters through the wringer in each volume. Top yourself. That's what the most successful series writers do. Their readers—and their characters—feel the difference.

BEYOND SELF

An inner journey is a self-discovery, but it can and should be about more than healing, relationships, and self-acceptance. We each have journeys in everything from our sense of fashion to our understanding of God.

What do you know about people that you didn't one year ago? What suddenly makes sense about the way the world works? What did your father teach you that still holds true? What did you learn in college that's dead wrong? What about your faith is painful to admit? When systems and philosophies let you down, what do you hold onto? How has the purpose of your life become clear?

Do those questions feel like hard work to answer? They are. But they're important because when it comes down to it, our deepest search is for meaning. Is it too much to send your characters on the same search? No. The quest for meaning is the ultimate inner journey.

In manuscripts, the quest for meaning is often saved for a summation at the end of a story. That's fine, but the need to understand the purpose of one's life can be planted early and developed throughout. Rebecca Stott's intellectual thriller *Ghostwalk* (2007) does this. It's the story of a writer, Lydia Brooke, who agrees to complete the manuscript of an historian friend whose body was found floating in the watery fens around Cambridge, England, with a glass prism clutched in her hand. The manuscript is about Isaac Newton's involvement with alchemy, but as Lydia digs into it, the story ties into a trio of Cambridge murders in Newton's time, which in turn link to killings in the present day.

It would be sufficient to simply spin this out as a past-present mystery story, with an Isaac Newton connection to give the cover copy extra gloss. But Stott doesn't neglect to give Lydia plenty of inner conflict and a mind that yearns for understanding. Early in the novel, Lydia is questioned by a detective in the functional Parkside Police Station. Later, she considers what she ought to have said:

> How do you tell him that you think there's a link between a female scholar found drowned in a river in Cambridge and a man who fell down a staircase nearby three hundred years earlier? Not a simple causal relationship but something as delicate as a web, one of those fine skeins you see around the tips of grass stems in the spring when the dew is heavy.
>
> A crow has just flown off my study roof, launched itself into the air to my left down over the garden, just as the right-hand corner of my map of Cambridge has curled itself noisily away from the wall. The syncopated sounds of the scurrying crows' feet on roof tiles and the curling of old paper is enough to make one think that there might be something else in the room beside me as I write. Which of you restless people is it? What do you want with my story?
>
> No. If Elizabeth were here she would say that history is less like a skein of silk and more like a palimpsest—time layered upon

time so that one buried layer leaks into the one above. Or like a
stain in an old stone wall that seeps through the plaster.

How does history relate to us? How do we tell its story? What is it that its
human subjects want us to see? What is our responsibility to them? How
do we discern truth when it's as wispy and delicate as a spider's web in a
grassy field? If the past is stained, it seeps through to the present. It demands an inquiry. Stott in this passage is grappling with the meaning not
only of history itself but with the necessity of telling its secrets. The symbolism (see chapter seven) of crows and a warped map of Cambridge add
associative meaning. This is heavy stuff for the beginning of a crime novel,
but it elevates the tone and asserts the story's significance. From the outset, Lydia is searching not just for answers to unsolved murders but for
the meaning of it all.

Push your protagonist's inner journey all the way to its ultimate destination. After all, the point of creating an inner journey is not just to transform characters, but to transform readers. When you do, your purpose as
a storyteller is almost fulfilled.

But your job is not done. A life plumbed is satisfying, especially for fiction writers whose intent is primarily literary. What makes a novel worthwhile, though, goes beyond the reality it creates and the emotions it stirs. It's
also the experience it enacts. And experience that's made up only of emotions will be only half effective. To achieve its full power, a story needs events.

⟨21ST CENTURY TOOLS⟩

EMOTIONAL LANDSCAPE

- Breathe. Lean back. Now, what feeling are you most afraid to put on the page? Get it down. To whom in the story does that feeling belong? Give it.
- What makes you blissfully happy? See that happiness as an object. What about it is familiar? What about it is wonderfully strange? Surprise your protagonist with that object, a gift.
- What emotion is new in your life? In what scene can your protagonist feel that, too? Get busy.
- In your current scene, what's the strongest emotion? Why is it welcome? Why not? What's good about it? What's utterly wrong?
- Pick a scene. What's the strongest emotion your point-of-view (POV) character feels? Write down three secondary emotions. Delete the primary emotion; keep the secondary ones.
- Find a moment when your protagonist feels nothing in particular. Look around. Pick something. Whatever it is, note two conflicting feelings your protagonist has about it. Add them.
- What does your protagonist do? Interview someone of the same profession. Ask, "What's a feeling you experience in this line of work that doesn't occur in others?" Add it in your manuscript.

RESTRAINT VS. EXPOSITION

- Pick a passage of exposition, one in which there's a loud feeling. Delete it. Evoke that emotion through actions alone.

- Pick a small moment, when something tiny happens. Write down every feeling your protagonist has about that. Go deeper. What does it mean or epitomize? How does it sum up life? Weave a passage. Something small becomes big.

OBVIOUS VS. NUANCED EMOTIONS

- Word search for neon emotions: rage, fear, loathing, desire, joy, grief. Delete. Replace those with emotions less expected.
- Is there a moment when your protagonist is numb, feeling nothing? Listen. Wait. When it's safe, what does your protagonist say first? Start there. Don't stop until your protagonist has dumped everything that's inside.
- In the story overall, what's the dominant, overriding emotion that your protagonist feels? If your protagonist were mute, what would she physically do to express what's inside? Add that.

CONFLICTING FEELINGS AND INTERNAL CONFLICT

- Pick any moment in your manuscript. What is your POV character feeling? Write down a contrasting or conflicting feeling that's also true at this moment. Add it.
- What does your protagonist most want? What's the opposite of that? Can your protagonist want both things? When?
- Pick a moment when your protagonist wants the opposite of what he normally wants. What does he do to go the other way? Do the same in two more places.
- When does your protagonist reject what he most wants? What's the biggest way in which he can throw it away or quit? (Make sure he can never get it back or return.)

DOWNWARD ARC

- What's your protagonist's worst habit, weakness, or blind spot? Why is she unable to control it? When does she first try—and fail?

- When is your protagonist's defect most embarrassing? Who notices, yet says nothing?

- What's the worst thing the defect can cost your protagonist? Make him pay the price.

- How does your protagonist know she has bottomed out? What's the most miserable, degrading sign? What's the first thing she then does differently?

SECRETS, SURPRISES, MISTAKES

- What has your protagonist never told anyone? What was his worst mistake? When in the story is he most wrecked, broken, and done? Have him now disclose the truth.

- To whom would your protagonist least like to confess? That's her confessor.

- What secret is your protagonist keeping? Who is keeping one from your protagonist? Spill the truth at the worst possible time.

- Pick a character other than your protagonist. What would your protagonist never, ever guess about this character? Spring that surprise.

- Whom is your protagonist afraid to let down? What is the sacred trust between them? What would cause your protagonist to break it? Break it.

SHAME

- Of what are you most ashamed? Describe that feeling without naming it. Now, when in your story is your protagonist most ashamed? Adapt your passage for your protagonist.

- What's the worst thing your protagonist does? Whom does it hurt? How? Work backwards. Set it up to hurt even more.

- Who forces your protagonist to confront her shame? How? How do we know, without being told, that your protagonist has forgiven herself?

HEALING

- What's your protagonist's deepest childhood hurt? What detail does she remember best from that incident? Plant that detail at three other times.

- There's something your protagonist can't let go. What's the deeper reason for that? Who knows that reason before your protagonist does?

- What's something that your protagonist doesn't yet know about the most hurtful person in her life? When will she find that out? How?

RECONCILE WITH THE PAST

- Who does your protagonist most need to forgive? What event puts that past wrong in perspective? What symbolizes letting go?

THE INNER JOURNEY

- What's the hardest action your protagonist will have to perform? Make it the one action that your protagonist has sworn never to do.

- What's the most important thing your protagonist needs to know about himself? Give him five good reasons not to care. Tear each one down, step by step.

- What truth does your protagonist cling to the hardest? Reinforce it three times. Then destroy it. It's wrong.

- Who does your protagonist hate the most? Reinforce it three times, or more. When does she discover she's mistaken? How?

- What's your protagonist's greatest hope? Build it three times. How is it naïve? What makes her realize that? Why does she let it go? What replaces that hope?
- What's your protagonist's highest principle? What cemented it? Find three ways and times it serves. How is he wrong? What brings that home? What new principle is learned?
- Where does your protagonist most want to go? What does that destination represent? Make the journey impossible in six ways. Then arrive. What's disappointing? What exceeds expectations? What has the journey itself revealed?
- What person matters most to your protagonist? Deepen that commitment three times. Then force a breach. Ruin that relationship. What's lost? What's gained? Repair—or not.

TURNING INTO EVENTS

- What are five stages on your protagonist's journey to self-knowledge? Create one event to dramatize each stage.

FAMILY AND FRIENDS

- Who changes because your protagonist does? Work backwards. Find three ways for that other character to resist that change, or to celebrate the status quo.
- Who changes in a way your protagonist doesn't like or want? Give that other character three actions to show his change underway.

SERIES CHARACTERS

- In this book, what enrages your series protagonist? What's the worst thing he'll have to do? What does she fear above all? What personal truth is painful to learn? What principle is at risk? Build in five steps the outrage, loathing, fear, resistance, or commitment. Push. Test. Go to extremes. Go beyond.

MEANING

- What larger truth does your protagonist learn? Earlier in the story, plant three clues.
- What puzzle is solved? List the pieces. Scatter them earlier. Hide them. Disguise them. Hand them to others. What event unlocks the solution? How?
- What's one thing your protagonist hates as the story opens? By the end, have your protagonist love that same thing. (Or vice versa.)
- At the novel's outset, how does your protagonist define her purpose in life? How is it different at the end?
- How have you changed over the past year? What's the biggest way in which a lifelong friend would see that change without being told? Give that to your protagonist.
- What's the biggest insight you've gained while writing this novel? Give that insight to your protagonist.

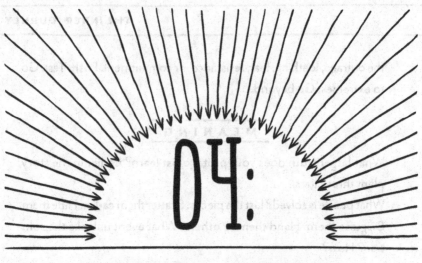

04:
THE OUTER JOURNEY

EVENTS AND THEIR IMPACT

Here's a litmus test for what you value most as a fiction writer: What do you feel when I say this word: Plot? If your insides relax, then you probably see your stories as composed of external events: fun to invent, challenging to arrange, necessary to strengthen.

If your insides tense up or you feel any degree of distaste or resistance, then you probably see your stories as primarily internal: the journey of a character, a reflection of lived experience, an insight into the truth of things. You may see plot as a four-letter word, or perhaps loathe it somewhat like partial differential equations, stuff you need to fathom in order to pass calculus but impossible to understand.

If you are tempted to skip this chapter, either because you feel you've already got this plot thing down pat or because story mechanics make you faintly nauseated, don't. Commercial storytellers often have a lot yet to learn about what makes a plot not just gripping but also powerful. Literary novelists frequently need to get comfortable with creating strong outward expressions of their characters' inner journeys.

Another difference in authors, whether commercial or literary in inclination, is in their approach to crafting a manuscript. Some plan it out, others intuit their way through. Outline writers get closer to the finished product in early drafts but can miss opportunities to explore their story's scenic avenues and dark alleys. Organic and intuitive writers tend to need more drafts, which are often radically different, and may wind up with a manuscript more original and unexpected in its form but also less tight, sharply focused, or smartly marching.

Both approaches have strengths and shortcomings. What's important is not to adopt a method that's unnatural—if you hate writing outlines, then don't bother—but instead to recognize the ways in which your approach will leave you shortchanged and make sure that you compensate.

Plot-driven storytellers often imagine they've got it licked. Plot will carry you through. A fast-moving, forward-driving story that readers can't put down trumps all other considerations. Keep 'em hooked and you're good. Character-driven storytellers, by contrast, tend to think that if they simply get it right—stun readers with a rendering of what's true—the emotional impact of a novel will put it over.

Both beliefs are mistaken. Clever twists and turns are only momentarily attention-grabbing. Relentless forward-driving action, high tension, and cliffhangers do serve to keep readers' eyeballs on the page but don't necessarily engage their hearts. By the same token, a dutifully rendered reality (reviewers call such writing "closely observed") may cause readers to catch their breath once in a while but the effect doesn't last long. Not enough is happening, and when it does it feels underwhelming. How then can commercial novelists construct plots that have true power? How can literary writers conjure events that give their work long-lasting effect?

The answer in all cases is to create events of enormous impact. If an event is external, excavate its inner meaning. If a moment is internal, push it out the door and make it do something large, real, permanent, and hard to miss. Whatever your assignment, you won't find it easy. It's not natural to you, since your tendency is to hold back.

EVENTS THAT STIR AND SURPRISE

Strong story events are surprising, emotional, and revealing, and enact permanent change. Weak story events are foreseeable, zipped up, and empty, and leave in place the story's status quo. Most manuscripts have plenty of the latter and little of the former. It needn't be that way.

Plot-driven writers are not necessarily masters of surprise. How many detective stories have you read where the plot lumbers along, ostensibly "building" but actually just spinning its wheels? How many romance novels merely churn, repeating over and over the same clash between hero and heroine? Have you ever seen a plot development coming a mile away? Do you ever finish a novel feeling that things turned out exactly as you expected?

I thought so.

A surprising story event (or, if you prefer, plot development) counters expectations. Think about that. The key word isn't counter, but expectations. In a way you're playing a game with your readers. Hey folks, guess what's going to happen? But you're manipulating the game and misdirection is your secret skill.

In the story you're working on right now, what's the rabbit that's due to pop out of the hat next? What development or surprise lies immediately ahead? Let's say it's the discovery of a second murder victim. Okay. Work with this assumption: Your reader isn't going to be surprised a bit. Why not? Pretty much every mystery novel ever written drops a second body. You're up against a heavy load of reader expectations.

That's true of all types of fiction. If you're not using a genre formula as a template, you may imagine that your reader can't possibly see where you're going. But you're wrong. All stories at their beginnings signal their intentions, their underlying values, and the outcomes for which we should hope. That signal is sometimes called *the promise to the reader* or *the contract with the reader.* If your main character is on a journey, sure enough he'll arrive. If your character is young in an adult world, believe it, she will come of age. You're not surprising anyone. Not really. For that you have to lay some plans.

Engineering surprise starts with the event, then works backward to build a contrary expectation.

John Hart is a multiple Edgar-Award-winning novelist. His third novel, *The Last Child* (2009), is an enormously puzzling mystery built around a boy, Johnny Merrimon, whose twin sister, Alyssa, disappeared when he was thirteen. A year later everyone has given up: the police, his shattered mother, and his unfeeling father, who left the family. But Johnny isn't giving up. He has a map. And a bike. And a list. It's a list of the six known sex offenders in the county. One by one he's visiting their houses.

Then another schoolgirl, Tiffany Shore, disappears. Against the wishes of police detective Clyde Hunt, Johnny plans to monitor the six offenders on his list. One of them probably took Alyssa, too, and he's going to find out who. Johnny is a warrior, an imaginary Indian chief. He takes courage from a native ritual he enacts using an eagle feather he took himself from a live eagle. Whoa. This kid's serious. And sure enough he finds Tiffany, who shoots her abductor before Johnny can learn more about Alyssa. But the truth lies deeper. It may be locked in the troubled mind of a black hermit, Levi Freemantle, or in a "hush arbor," a secret place deep in the woods where freed slaves practiced their native African religion. Johnny runs away. Meantime, Detective Hunt's investigation finally leads to a woodsy graveyard.

The first body unearthed in this graveyard is the novel's second biggest surprise: It's the body of Johnny's father, who died looking for Alyssa.

This discovery reverses the expectations of all: Hunt, Johnny's mother, and Hart's readers. But think about it: Discovery of a second body has come to be expected, right? But it is a surprise, though, because Hart has carefully led our expectations astray. Did Hart plan this or did the idea arise during the writing? I'll ask him sometime. It doesn't matter. The point is, even a routine second body can be a huge surprise . . . that is, if we are set up to *be* surprised. The method is manipulation of our beliefs.

By the way, did you notice I called the discovery of the body of Johnny's father the "second" biggest surprise in *The Last Child*? Ah. There's an even bigger surprise in store for you when you read this novel: the ultimate solution to the disappearance of Johnny's sister, Alyssa. Keep in mind the principle of misdirection. Who do you expect is Alyssa's killer? Hart knows what you're thinking because he's led you to think it. As a result, the truth that he probably planned all along is hidden in plain sight. (Read for yourself and see.)

Surprise is important, but it's only one aspect of creating events with impact. The second thing to work on is making sure that events stir readers' hearts.

Emotional impact can happen unplanned as you draft (always nice), or instead, you can design it. Work backward from a known event and ask, "How can I make this an explosion at the end of a long emotional fuse?" If that sounds too calculated for you, fine. Wait until you've finished your current draft. Look at the high points, the biggest and most dramatic events. What's the emotional impact of each? Is that impact as strong as it can be? In your mind it is, naturally enough, but what do your first readers say? If you're getting anything less than raves, there's work to do. The event itself doesn't need changing, but the path leading up to it does.

In *The Last Child*, the second body discovery makes clear that Johnny Merrimon's father did not abandon his family but was rather looking for his missing daughter. On whom does this revelation have an impact?

On his family, naturally, and John Hart doesn't ignore that. Hart is a cool stylist (see chapter eight), so he effectively shows the change in Johnny's mother in the novel's final pages: After a year of grief and addiction to painkillers, she buys a (symbolic) new house.

Certain trusty story events always produce emotional impact—for instance, the death of a beloved character or a heartfelt welcome home. You can't always count on that effect, though. Emotional impact isn't automatic. Sometimes you need to pause in your process and ask, "What do I want my reader to feel right here?" Whatever it is, you can work on it. Does that sound like manipulation of the reader? I call it effective writing. (More on this in chapter six.)

Still, if you're a writer of literary intent, everything I've been talking about may sound grotesque to you. What I'm suggesting is the cheapest kind of low-class trickery, antithetical to good writing because it's inorganic. It feels false and probably reads that way, too. If you're a writer who hates outlines, it probably also feels plain impossible to be so calculating. Who can plan anything in a novel?

So don't plan it, manipulate, or do anything else that offends you, but do recognize that your artistic sensibility pulls you away from strong feelings. It pushes you toward what is subtle, nuanced, and delicate, which can be another way of saying what is small, nebulous, and weak. Move readers faintly if you want to. Okay by me. But if that's all you do, the result will be a novel of light impact. For heavy impact, you need to go for strong effect.

It's all in the groundwork. A routine deceit can be a major betrayal. Love can be a delicious discovery or a force that swallows one whole. Fear can tap you in the dark or it can pounce like a beast that stalks your children.

To deliver a strong effect to your readers you've first got to give yourself permission to go big. Big feelings aren't bad; they're just big. We all have them. They're dramatic. They connect. The only time they don't is when they're false: rote, hackneyed, pasted on, or unearned. Think of them as primary emotions that take on unique hues in the heart of your main character. Love? Sure, but different this time. Rage? Never before like this one. Sorrow? Yes, but now utterly specific.

Whether you design an emotional inferno or simply fling a lighted match into a dry forest to see what will happen, the important thing is that the events in your story are on fire. A plot development is a nice accomplishment, but without emotional impact it's just something that happens. Emotional experiences are fine, too, but unless they're externalized in actions, they won't touch readers. They lack the kinetic force of the real.

EVENTS THAT REVEAL AND CHANGE

Literary writers can feel flummoxed by the whole externalization thing. How do you know when something should happen? How can you make something happen without it feeling forced and artificial? Action sounds like comic books. Isn't change where you're moving to rather than where you're dwelling? What if being stuck is the whole point?

Such worries are legitimate. Let's shift the vocabulary. Surprise is not a gimmick but rather a countering of expectations. Mining emotions doesn't always set off a tectonic shift, but should tilt the ground. Revealing facts or truths doesn't rob a climax, but instead build toward one. Change isn't a terminal event; it's an ongoing condition of life. Big things may not happen much in real life, but stories are the most effective when external events reflect, reverse, and magnify what's inside.

Go ahead. Make things happen. You've got a license, a double 0; it's your job. When to make an event? Any scene or discrete unit of a story will be stronger for one. Anything important that's internal can be externalized. Ask, "In this scene what can my character *do*? What is the *biggest thing* he can do? What does she *secretly* want to do? What won't others expect, least of all me? What is he avoiding or resisting? What can she do that will unintentionally show her (or others) what she's refusing to see?"

Jonathan Safran Foer's *Extremely Loud & Incredibly Close* (2005) is a novel of the aftermath of 9/11. Are you depressed yet? Wait, it gets worse. The novel's protagonist is a precocious boy, Oskar Schell, who compulsively creates inventions that are mostly useless, always imaginative, and frequently symbolic of his grief. His father died in the collapse of the Twin Towers. The subject of the novel is Oskar's unresolved grief.

Foer could easily have indulged himself in the three Rs of low-impact literary writing: reaction, reflection, and remembering. There's plenty of that in his novel, but Foer is also smart. He gives Oskar something to do. In his father's closet is a blue vase. In the vase is a small envelope. In the envelope is an oddly shaped key. On the envelope is written a word, "Black," someone's name. Because Oskar's father frequently left him secret messages and puzzles, Oskar decides this is one. Oskar needs to do something proactive in order not to die inside:

> That was kind of how I felt when I decided that I would meet every person in New York with the last name Black. Even if it was relatively insignificant, it was something, and I needed to do something, like sharks, who die if they don't swim, which I know about.

That's not the last externalization in Foer's novel. Oskar does find the owner of the key, which also unlocks the mystery of why his father left his tuxedo unhung in his closet. At last it's time for him to let his father go. He digs up his father's coffin (it's empty, of course) with the help of a character called "the renter." The renter also has something to bury, letters he wrote to a child he abandoned before birth, and so, together, they symbolically release the past.

That's not all. Foer has a few more surprises in store. Throughout the novel he has led us to believe that Oskar's mother has gone dead inside. She barely has anything to do. She never questions Oskar when he says simply that he's going "out." But Oskar has not been on a solo quest. Thanks to one of the Blacks, he realizes that his mother knew what he was doing. She not only approved but phoned ahead to the Blacks so that he would be expected. She has loved and cared for him all along. This realization tugs at our hearts all the more because Foer led us to believe that the opposite was true. Is that manipulation or simply a mother's love in the face of enormous grief?

I call it beautiful.

When the actions you create come from inside a character, you needn't worry that they'll feel artificial. They won't because they're active expressions of actual needs. If it helps, think of events as symbolic. Give them hidden psychological significance. Use them to challenge your readers: *Is this what you would do?* Better still, use them to upset readers: *That's exactly what I wouldn't do!* Beautiful.

Avoidance and delay aren't actions. Suffering is a negative number. Adding up negative numbers doesn't give you a positive number, just a bigger negative. At any given moment, make your characters do something. It's stronger than if something is done to them.

What if the moment is a lifting of spirits, fresh appreciation, dawning suspicion, growing dread, dying hope, surrender to the inevitable, or any other stage of an unfolding development that is by nature inactive? What's the role of actions when there is no action? While it's possible and sometimes clever to capture on the page that which is intangible (see chapter seven), for the most part the old adage remains true: showing is better than telling. At inactive moments, challenge yourself to remove from the page what a character is feeling. Even more, provoke your readers to apprehend whatever it is merely through what your character says and does.

That's active, artful writing. Now, let's do a spot check. After reading what's above, are you still tempted to fall back on evocative atmosphere? Swishing trees and lengthening shadows speak in a whisper. Gunshots are loud. Find their equivalent at this moment in your story and pull the trigger. You may feel uncomfortable, but only until you get the reaction of your critique group. They'll approve, just as you do when other writers quit trying to make story out of poetry and instead make characters do something that readers can visualize.

Plot-driven writers tend to be better at creating external events and putting their characters into action. But that doesn't mean all action in commercial novels packs a punch. Some of the biggest explosions I've ever read have been some of the dullest reading I've ever endured. Action by itself is empty. To have impact it must reveal something about a character. To do that you can't settle for just writing down reactive emotions. Actions always have a hidden psychological significance and maybe even a meaning that has far-reaching echoes.

Think about this: You pick up a glass of wine and set it down again without taking a sip. What does that say? Depending on the context, it could say that you're: not having fun, not playing that game, not ready, too ready, toying or teasing, cutting the crap, indecisive, making up your mind, or any number of other possibilities. But whatever the truth underlying that simple act of not sipping, it's revealed.

Extrapolated, that's what makes a given story event linger in memory: what it illuminates about the character involved. That in turn requires the author (that's you) to think about what it is at any given moment that you want to reveal. Do you have something to reveal? Not always. Not enough. Pages and pages of manuscript can go by in which we don't learn a blessed new thing about its characters. We may keep reading for other reasons, but scrimping storytelling will not stick in your mind.

When you think about it, the dynamic we're discussing is wholly human. It's enacted in our own lives. Was there a moment in your life when you realized that you'd never be the same or that you'd never again do things in the same old way? Did you ever feel the direction of your life permanently shifting? Were you moving a tassel from one side of your graduation cap to the other? Were you looking at a diamond ring on your finger? Was there a newborn in a crib that was empty the day before?

Maybe you were kicking the door of your steaming, broken-down wreck of a car by the side of a highway, cursing your cheapskate spouse who against all promises refuses to spend the money it takes to maintain important things like a marriage? Perhaps you slammed down on your desk the fifth redraft of a legal motion and knew with iron certainty in your gut that you simply couldn't go on helping shitty corporations keep skirting the law and avoiding the fallout from their own stupid mistakes?

Change can occur at any moment, if you let it. To put it another way, any moment in life (or a story) is an opportunity for change waiting to be used. Not all self-revelations are positive, naturally. Some are shameful discoveries: letdowns that, wonderfully, can lead to change.

Lev Grossman's *The Magicians* (2009) was hailed as a Harry Potter for grown-ups. Its central character, Quentin Coldwater, has more in common with Holden Caulfield than Harry Potter. At Brakebills College, an upstate New York school for wizards, Quentin finds that learning spells is boring. Quentin messes up his romantic life, too, over and over making the same mistakes. Eventually he and his friends Eliot, Janet, and Julia transport to a genuine magical realm called Fillory for some real adventure, but honestly they're a bunch of screw-ups. They blow their big chance and fail to appreciate the magic and beauty around them. Nevertheless, they become Fillory's kings and queens.

The sequel, *The Magician King* (2011), finds Quentin and co. enjoying the party life of monarchs, but in truth it's gotten kind of dull:

> And how often did he get a chance to put his royal person at risk? When was the last time he even cast a spell? His life wasn't exactly fraught with peril. They lay around on cushions all day and ate and drank their heads off all night. Lately whenever he sat down some untoward interaction had been happening between his abdomen and his belt buckle. He must have gained fifteen pounds since he took the throne. No wonder kings looked so fat in pictures. One minute you're Prince Valiant, the next you're Henry VIII.

For kicks, Quentin and his crew embark on a quest . . . only to find themselves transported from Fillory back to Chesterton, Massachusetts, the utterly mundane town from which Quentin came, and then after a while back again. Things happen. People die. Julia is raped by a god, but it's sort of anti-climactic, lasting only seven or ten minutes. It's, you know, that kind of adventure. At the end, Quentin has to pay a price, which is the loss of his crown, but that too feels anti-climactic:

> Quentin had been braced for devastation, but when it came he didn't feel anything at all. That was what they were taking, and they would take it. Had taken it. He didn't feel any different. It was all very abstract, kingliness. He faced the others, but none of them looked at him any differently. He took a deep breath.
> "Well," he said stupidly. "Easy come."

You might think that Lev Grossman was merely writing parody, a kind of anti-Harry Potter full of anti-heroes and ironic detachment. If so, his novels would be just send-ups. But they're not. Quentin and his fuck-up friends have grabbed readers harder than that, as the many glowing reviews and strong sales prove. How does Grossman pull off that trick? He does it by giving his characters heart; or perhaps it's truer to say that he gives his own heart to his characters. At the end of *The Magician King*, Quentin finds that his adventures have not been empty:

> But something had changed inside him, too. He didn't understand it yet, but he felt it. How was it that now that he'd lost everything, he felt more like a king than he had before? He waved to the empty square, like he used to wave to the court at Fillory.

Grossman thus demonstrates that even the disappointing events of the life of an anti-hero can bring about self-revelations, which in turn lead to change.

When story events reveal and change characters, that's good storytelling. When story events also cause us to see and recognize ourselves, that's great storytelling. All novelists want their work to portray universal human truths. What's less easily understood is that universal truths arise from story situations and actions that are completely unique.

Teenagers feel trapped. They long for freedom. This universal adolescent feeling was epitomized in William Sleator's existential young adult classic *House of Stairs* (1974), a premise wonderfully revived and refreshed in James Dashner's *The Maze Runner* (2009). As in Sleator's novel, kids are mysteriously dropped into a puzzling nowhere place. They must survive and learn truths about themselves. In *The Maze Runner*, the nowhere place is a glade where boys arrive by elevator at the rate of one a month with no memory of who they are or why they're there. Surrounding the glade is a vast maze, a potential escape route that morphs and throws obstacles that make it impossible to leave.

The gate to the Maze shuts every night, and you sure don't want to be caught outside after curfew. It's inhabited by nasty enforcer creatures called Grievers. The novel's hero is a boy called only Thomas, who late in the story selflessly puts himself through a painful quasi-death termed the Changing in order to recover his memory. What he learns is awful: The Maze has no exit. It's a survival-of-the-fittest test designed by a dystopian government for yet-to-be revealed reasons. The revelations grow worse. The Maze was designed by Thomas himself, along with Teresa, the only girl ever to arrive in the Glade. Thus, the trap of the title is a torment of teenagers' own making.

See the metaphor? *The Maze* has a science fictional underpinning, explained in the remainder of Dashner's trilogy, *The Scorch Trials* (2010) and *The Death Cure* (2011), but its larger meaning isn't lost on young readers. Sure, the world is a test written and rigged by adults, but it's kids who succumb and even collaborate in creating the oppressive conditions of this world. It's a message as old as William Golding's *Lord of the Flies* (1954) and as fresh as the latest suicide provoked by bullying.

Ordinary and expected human behavior has low impact on readers. We tune out what's numbingly familiar. But when something unusual happens, or a character does something that we don't expect, we pause, take note, ponder, process, and come to terms with it. We have to. Universal truth isn't a nodding agreement that arrives automatically; it's a concurrence that you force readers into when you push them out of their comfort zone. To do that you, in turn, must push yourself to create story events that undeniably dramatize the truths you hold in your heart.

THE HIERARCHY OF EXTERNALIZATIONS

Externalize. Strongly. What's inside can be turned outward. Internalize. Powerfully. What happens outwardly has inner meaning. Both externalization and mining events for their significance are critical. They're the opposite sides of the same coin: high-impact storytelling.

As you can see, however, when it comes to story events, there's a hierarchy of effectiveness. Visible actions are stronger than internal moments. Acting is stronger than reacting. Surprise is better than playing out the obvious. Changing the game is stronger than leaving in place the status quo; stronger still is changing the players themselves in unforeseen ways.

How can you be sure you're doing those things? Well, you can't do them by slogging through successive drafts, cutting, changing words, and hoping for the best. You've got to seize your story like a potter grips clay and shape it. You've got to examine it according to higher criteria and go to work.

Start with each scene, chapter, or other unit you use to break up your manuscript. Rate the following: external actions, expectations vs. what happens, discovery, and change. Or have someone else do it. Making a scene "better," "tighter," or "punchier" is an okay intention, but it's imprecise. A more reliable path to high impact is to focus on the effect you seek. You'll get it by directing expectations, building an emotional roadbed, working out what your characters will discover about themselves, and making sure that at the end something is distinctly different.

Needless to say, it's a good idea to design scenes that way from the outset. Not everyone can do that, or wants to. No worries. The process doesn't matter, but the outcome does. Once you've got the knack of devising strong story events, you can progress to some cool, sophisticated, and fun story techniques, the kind of stuff used by story masters.

TURNS, TWISTS, AND DEEP DARK SECRETS

Earlier I said that twists and turns are momentary effects that may seize readers' attention but don't always engage them emotionally. True enough, but they're still pretty cool. Can they be planned? Sure. A turn in a story is an unexpected happening, one that changes the readers' idea of what's going on. It shifts expectations of where we're going next.

Kate Morton's international best-seller *The Forgotten Garden* (2009) is a multi-strand past-and-present story that begins with the mysterious arrival in Australia of a little girl, all alone, on an ocean liner in 1913. She knows only that she was put on the ship by a woman called The Authoress, but why? The Authoress, we eventually learn, is an Edwardian writer of dark fairy tales named Eliza Makepeace. Her story is one of the novel's three principle narrative lines.

We first meet Eliza as a London urchin, her mother recently deceased, who has been taken in by an unscrupulous foster-mother with the deliciously evocative name Mrs. Swindell. Eliza scavenges on the streets. The coins and meager treasures she finds are immediately surrendered to Mrs. Swindell as payment. One day a pair of do-gooders arrives to take Eliza to a workhouse. She struggles but the tussle is interrupted:

> "Stop immediately."
>
> All sound evaporated as Eliza, Mrs. Swindell and the two Misses Sturgeon turned to see whence the words came. Standing in the open doorway was a man dressed all in black. Behind him, a shiny carriage. Children were gathered around it, touching the

wheels and marveling at the glowing lanterns up front. The man allowed his gaze to pass over the tableau before him.

"Miss Eliza Makepeace?"

Eliza nodded in a jerky fashion, unable to find words. Too dismayed that her point of escape was now blocked to wonder at the identity of this stranger who knew her name.

"Daughter of Georgiana Mountrachet?" He handed a photograph to Eliza. It was Mother, much younger, dressed in the fine clothing of a lady. Eliza's eyes widened. She nodded, confused.

"I am Phineas Newton. On behalf of Lord Mountrachet of Blackhurst Manor, I have come to collect you. To bring you home to the family estate."

It's a reversal-of-fortune moment that would make Dickens proud. Although Eliza's apparent rescue will prove less lucky than hoped, in the moment it's a huge turnabout. Attentive readers may wonder if the elevation of a starving orphan may be an over-used device, and maybe it is. But it stops Eliza's story in its tracks and sends her in an altogether new direction.

The author, of course, knows what will later happen to Eliza at Blackhurst Manor. It's central to the mystery of the unattended little girl who arrives in Brisbane thirteen years later. If you think about it, though, Eliza's story could have had any sort of beginning at all. Although the story requires that Eliza's mother be estranged from her family, and be deceased, in fact Eliza might have been living comfortably. Her hardscrabble circumstances provide contrast. The turn this represents, then, is one engineered to feel more like a turn than it really is.

If *turns* are unexpected things that happen, *twists* are things done by unexpected people. Role reversals, as in betrayal, are one surefire way to create a twist. There are others. Were you shocked to learn that your Uncle Joe plays the banjo? Did your jaw drop when Aunt Josephine said, "Didn't anyone ever tell you that Grandma was a stripper?" Skills, knowledge, and back-story information can be saved up. Assign that stuff to unlikely characters and you have a mini-twist.

Twists can also be small, unexpected moments that catch the reader by surprise. When they do, ordinary scenes can pop alive. There are several such moments in *The Last Detective* (2003) by best-selling crime writer Robert Crais, whose series detective Elvis Cole is a magnet for trouble. In *The Last Detective*, Cole is spending a couple of days with his girlfriend's eight-year-old son, Ben, when the boy is kidnapped, not for ransom but for revenge. As the hunt for the boy unfolds, Ben is buried alive in a plastic box with a tube for air. Ben cuts his way out of the box using a military medal—a Silver Star—that Elvis gave him. He nearly escapes but is recaptured by the bad guys, one of whom uncharacteristically shows his admiration for Ben's bravery:

> Mike ran his hands over Ben's legs, then searched Ben's pockets and came out with the Silver Star. He held it up by the ribbon.
>
> "Did Cole give you this?"
>
> The best Ben could do was nod.
>
> Mike dangled the medal in front of Mazi and Eric.
>
> "He cut his way out with this. See how the points are dull? You fucked up. You should've searched him."
>
> "It's a fuckin' medal, not a knife."
>
> Mike grabbed Eric's throat with such speed that Ben didn't see his hand move. Their faces were only inches apart with Ben sandwiched between them.
>
> "Fuck up again, I'll put you down."
>
> Eric's voice gurgled.
>
> "Yes, sir."
>
> "Keep your shit tight. You're better than this."
>
> Eric tried to answer again, but couldn't. Mike squeezed even harder.
>
> Mazi gripped Mike's arm.
>
> "Ewe ahr keeleeng heem."

>Mike let go. He considered the Silver Star again, then pushed
>it into Ben's pocket.
>"You earned it."

Secrets are powerful, especially when revealed. Keeping secrets is hard. That's true in novel writing, too. Beginners are prone to blab too soon. Pros delight in withholding key facts from readers. When that withheld information is shameful, shocking, or contrary to our expectations, so much the better. Dishing it out will make for delicious dining.

Tatiana de Rosnay's international best-seller *Sarah's Key* (2007) revolves around a terrible event in the history of the Occupation of France by Germany during World War II, the Vel' d'Hiv, short for the Vélodrome d'Hiver, a roundup of French Jews by the Paris police who held them in a cycling velodrome under horrid conditions for a week before shipping them to Auschwitz. The novel is a past-and-present story told from the points of view of a ten-year-old Jewish girl, the titular Sarah Starzynski, and in the present day an American journalist, Julia Jarmond, who writes for an English language magazine, *Seine Scenes*. Julia is assigned a story on the sixtieth anniversary of Vel' d'Hiv.

The WWII story thread relates the terrifying nighttime removal of Sarah and her family from their apartment in 1942. Sarah's little brother hides in a hidden cupboard in their room. Sarah is taken away but carries the key to the cupboard. She expects to return within a day, but that is not to be. What happens to the boy locked in the cupboard is a mystery central to the story. Meanwhile in 2002, Julia researches the Vel' d'Hiv while her French architect husband, Bertrand, sets about renovating for them an apartment in the Marais district vacated by his elderly grandmother.

You probably can guess that this apartment is the same one occupied in 1942 by Sarah and her family. What's not obvious, and a shocking secret when finally revealed late in the novel, is that Bertrand's family not only acquired the apartment long ago for a pittance, his grandmother knew the entire story of the Starzynski family, about the brother locked in the cupboard, and for sixty years kept the secret to sanitize their ownership of the apartment. She thus guarded the family from guilt but also, unfortunately, kept Sarah's family in America from knowing the truth about Sarah's troubled life and the reason for her tragic suicide.

Secrets are poisonous. They corrupt. They have an evil life of their own. They can stretch across decades, even centuries, and destroy reputations, relationships, and lives. They must not fester. For all to be right, they must come to light. Break silence. Do not keep secrets—except in your fiction, where their corrosive influence and dark gravity make for high drama.

When working with secrets, pick fragmentary indicators of what you're withholding and drop them in. Don't explain. You may worry that readers will guess what you're concealing, but mostly they won't. A big reveal is most effective when it provokes not only, "Oh, wow!" but also "Of course!" Make readers kick themselves for not seeing, you sly dog.

COMEBACK AND REDEMPTION

As I was writing this chapter (in July 2011), the US government was engaged in a bruising deadlock over raising the national debt ceiling. Remember that? Tea Party conservatives stubbornly brought the US to the brink of default with uncompromising demands for spending cuts and a refusal to allow anything that could be remotely construed as a tax increase.

By the end of the process, the nation was disgusted. The eleventh-hour compromise pleased no one. On the evening of August 1, the House of Representatives crawled through its voting. The mood was sour and tense until the final minutes. Then a miracle happened. Into the chamber, unannounced and unsteady, came Rep. Gabrielle Giffords of Arizona, who the previous January had been shot in the head.

She voted. On Twitter she said, "The Capitol looks beautiful tonight. I am honored to be at work."

The chamber erupted in applause as she arrived. The whole nation was lifted. In one second it became possible to look forward in hope. Rep. Giffords reminded the nation of an eternal truth.

We can come back from anything.

The uplift of a moment like that gets to us extra hard because we previously sank so low. Fiction writers take note. Sink your characters low. Bring them back with high symbolism. Works every time.

In your work-in-progress, what's your protagonist's biggest mistake? Work backward. Build your protagonist's commitment to do things right. Now line up what it will cost your protagonist to do something wrong. Who will be crushed when your protagonist later screws up? Make that person's high regard of your protagonist utterly important. What's something that your protagonist cannot afford to lose? Tie it in. What principle will your protagonist later violate? Make it foundational. Make the screw up itself bigger, more public. Make it so that your protagonist's closest friends look away, ashamed. Throw your protagonist into quicksand. Apologies and backtracking only make the error worse.

The comeback is not just a return; it's redemption. Your protagonist must atone. Give him work to do. Impose humility. What's the lesson? What's the biggest thing he must do to show that he has changed? Again work backward. Focus on the action that will show change. Plant it, make it important in your story world, rehearse it in smaller ways—which is to say, build up its symbolic value.

Deep into *A Feast for Crows* (2005), the fourth volume of George R. R. Martin's vast fantasy epic *A Song of Ice and Fire,* a knight smacks another knight in the face. The reason is that the second knight was making fun of a third knight, a female. This female knight is large as any man but is ugly and awkward. The first knight defends her honor. She is after all a knight, a brave and noble one, which her defender has seen firsthand.

Now, this might be a passing moment in a long epic, a trifling incident, but the man so sensitive to another knight's honor is Jaime Lannister. If you're following the series, you know that Jaime is utterly amoral. For years he has carried on an incestuous affair with his twin sister, a queen, and has even sired her three children. Earlier he killed the king he was sworn to protect. He's known as Kingslayer, trusted by no one, reviled by all.

Jaime? Jaime Lannister? Defending the honor of someone else? The turnaround of this most loathsome (if handsome) of characters is but one of thousands of surprises in Martin's singular sequence. But Jaime is changing. The female knight in question is Brienne of Tarth, who in the previous volume, *A Storm of Swords* (2000), is charged with delivering Jaime, a prisoner, to King's Landing to be exchanged for two sisters, Sansa and Arya Stark. The journey is perilous. Jaime has several chances to escape, but Brienne's strength, courage, and commitment impress him. He rescues her more than once. And then, randomly, Jaime has his sword hand chopped off. His identity is shattered. In the wake of this life-changing event he begins to reform, seeking the true values of his training and solemn pledges.

In *A Feast for Crows*, the knight that Jaime smacks in the face is Ronnet Connington, who once was betrothed to Brienne. That Jaime defends Brienne against one who was supposed to love her is ironic. Even better, though, is the way in which it's done: Jaime hits Connington in the face with his replacement golden hand. The strike is doubly satisfying for its symbolic value. Like I say, this could have been a small passing incident; instead it's a loaded moment that wonderfully shows one man's comeback and, in case you missed it, marks it with a lustrous symbol.

Still later in *A Feast for Crows*, Jaime has another chance to show that he's changed. After years of succumbing to his twin sister Cersei's erotic spell, she once again calls on him for help:

> There was a rap upon his door. "See who that is, Peck."
> It was Riverrun's old maester, with a message clutched in his lined and wrinkled hand. Vyman's face was as pale as the new-

fallen snow. "I know," Jaime said, "there has been a white raven from the Citadel. Winter has come."

"No, my lord. The bird was from King's Landing. I took the liberty . . . I didn't know . . ." He held the letter out.

Jaime read it in the window seat, bathed in the light of that cold winter morning. Qyburn's words were terse and to the point. Cersei's fevered and fervent. *Come at once*, she said. *Help me. Save me. I need you now as I never needed you before. I love you. I love you. I love you. Come at once.*

Vyman was hovering by the door, waiting, and Jaime sensed that Peck was watching too. "Does my lord wish to answer?" the maester asked, after a long silence.

A snowflake landed on the letter. As it melted, the ink began to blur. Jamie rolled the parchment up again, as tight as one hand would allow, and handed it to Peck. "No," he said. "Put this in the fire."

Jaime Lannister thus rejects the lover he has never been able to resist: his twin sister. As turnabouts go, this is huge. It's a series turning point and an effective surprise because for four volumes Jaime has heeded Cersei's siren call.

Uplift is a sweet moment in any story. It fills us with hope, inspires us with its courage. But there's work behind it, and that work belongs to you. But if you do it faithfully, your readers will love you for making your protagonist screw up.

ULTIMATE EVENTS

What's the last great ending you read? Need some time? If you do, I'm not surprised. Many endings are predictable, flat, and forgettable. We arrive on time, feel familiar feelings, and affirm easy truths. Even high-action novels can leave us strangely untested and unchanged. Literary characters frequently find resolution; they rarely triumph.

To some extent, the culmination of a novel is the sum of the conflicts you put in place: the main problem, the secondary plot layers, escalating inner conflict, the arc of change, irresolvable issues, timeless themes, and so on. Piling on problems and clearing them away is satisfying.

But 21st century fiction doesn't aim to be merely pleasing. Why just resolve when you can revolutionize? Why simply relieve when you can wring dry? Why wave readers away smiling when you can send them away staggering? Why not shoot for great endings?

How?

It takes some work. What's the thing your protagonist would never want to do? Where's the place she least wants to go? What is it that she is most afraid of losing? What's her deepest fear? What's the most impossible task? What sacrifice cannot be avoided? What, in this story, is total defeat? What does it mean, in this story, to die?

Do it. Go there. Take it away, permanently. Deliver the fear. Force the task. Remove all hope. Demand the sacrifice. Enact defeat. Wreck everything. Great endings are built of great climaxes: enormous feats, worst fears, tremendous losses, harrowing sacrifices, utter destruction.

Abraham Verghese's *Cutting for Stone* (2009) has enjoyed a long residency on the *New York Times* Best Sellers List. It's about twin brothers, Marion and Shiva Stone, conjoined at birth but later separated not only surgically but by the tumultuous events in their native Ethiopia and a femme fatale whom they both love. Sons of a vanished British surgeon and an Indian nun, the brothers both become surgeons as well. The story is largely Marion's. He emigrates to America where, finally, he reencounters his father, the femme fatale, and his brother, whose betrayal with the femme fatale originally propelled him away. Late in the story Marion is dying of liver failure brought about by hepatitis B (passed to him with symbolic logic by the femme fatale).

Marion needs a liver transplant, which is not easy to get but without which he will surely die. It's a moment of high stakes and high drama, which reaches its climax when Marion's brother, Shiva, selflessly suggests to their father that he perform a risky and at that time experimental graft using a portion of Shiva's own liver. Why would selfish Shiva do this? He explains:

> When he opened his eyes, he seemed for the first time since his arrival to be sad. He said, "Marion always thought that I never looked back. He saw me as always acting for myself. He was right. He would be surprised if I were to risk my life to donate part of my liver. It isn't rational. But . . . seeing that my brother might die, I have looked back. I have regrets.
>
> "If I was dying, if there was a chance he could save me, Marion would have pushed you to operate. That was his way. I never understood it before because it's irrational. But I understand it now." He glanced at Hema, then shouldered on.
>
> "I had no reason to think about this until I got here. But at his bedside . . . I realized if something happens to him, it happens to me, too. If I love myself, I love him, for we are one."

Commercial fiction also often enacts endings that are ostensibly exciting, but which do not wrench our hearts, force impossible change, or cost anything big. When commercial endings do wallop us, their effect on sales is huge.

Jim Butcher is a #1 *New York Times* best-selling author, having steadily built his following with his series about Chicago wizard-detective Harry Dresden. The twelfth in the series, *Changes* (2010), brings to a boil long-simmering conflicts between the powers that be in the paranormal world that co-exists with us clueless mundanes, the Red Court (vampire baddies) and the White Council (wizard good guys).

As the novel opens, Harry learns that he has a daughter, Maggie, by ex-girlfriend Susan Rodriguez. Maggie has been kidnapped. She will be sacrificed, he learns, to create a bloodlines curse that will wipe out many with one stroke, including Harry. Turning this situation around costs Harry plenty: his office building explodes, his home burns down, his car is crushed, he's paralyzed in a fall, he must sell himself to Mab (the Winter Queen), his allies become enemies, he duels to the death, he survives a hit squad, and after all that, he still hasn't saved his daughter.

The climactic battle at Chichén Itzá brings together almost every player and weapon in the series, and features a major last-minute betrayal as well as an enormous sacrifice: Susan makes herself a full vampire, the Red Court's newest, meaning that if she dies on the altar via a ritual knife, the Red Court will be destroyed forever. Harry thus faces a terrible choice. He can end the paranormal war once and for all, but to do so he must kill his daughter's mom for whom, he's discovered, he still has strong feelings. Here's how Butcher plays it:

> Everything in me screamed no. That this was not fair. That I should not have to do this. That no one should *ever* have to do this.
>
> But . . . I had no choice.
>
> I found myself picking Susan up with one hand. The little girl was curled into a ball with her eyes closed, and there was no time. I pushed her from the altar as gently as I could and let her fall to the floor, where she might be a little safer from the wild energies surging through the temple.
>
> I put Susan on the altar and said, "She'll be safe. I promise."
>
> She nodded at me, her body jerking and twisting in convulsions, forcing moans of pain from her lips. She looked terrified, but then she nodded.
>
> I put my left hand over her eyes.
>
> I pressed my mouth to hers, swiftly, gently, tasting the blood, and her tears, and mine.
>
> I saw her lips form the word, "Maggie . . ."
>
> And I . . .
>
> I used the knife.
>
> I saved a child.
>
> I won a war.
>
> God forgive me.

After a 400-page build up, not much is needed to sink in the enormity of the moment. Butcher lets the action itself wring our hearts. Harry wins but he also loses. He's accepted his role but it's hell. Regrets and sacrifice, unavoidable death and impossible change . . . this is the stuff of great endings; endings made even more dramatic by a long buildup in the middle that makes failure final and defeat certain.

Coming back from defeat isn't easy but, hey, there's always a way back. You know that because you've done it yourself. What was the worst moment of your entire life? Was it also the last moment? No. You recovered, learned, grew stronger, and, in time, came back. So can your characters.

Here's the place to indulge your flair for drama. What's the first ray of sunrise on a new day? What single act or circumstance will show that things are going to be different? Who turns back to your protagonist with fresh understanding? Who offers to help? Who's the *least likely person* to offer to help? What's the most meaningful gesture your protagonist can make? What can he fix? Whom can she repay? What are the most dramatic ways in which that could be done? What does it mean in this story to make it, arrive, win, turn around, triumph, be forgiven, go on? What symbolizes that? What's a reward that's undeserved? What's an outcome too wonderful to hope for? Make it big.

Many happy endings arrive without extreme effort or hard-won change, and so don't make us very happy. But when the journey has been more difficult than any reader could imagine, when failure is final and recovery impossible, then the turnaround is wondrous. Put your protagonist through that and I promise you'll connect powerfully with readers because the outer journey will have potent meaning.

⊸21ST CENTURY TOOLS⊸

SURPRISE

- Pick a scene. What's the outcome? Work backwards. Convince the reader that the outcome will be the opposite of what you've written.
- Pick a scene. What's the outcome? Now reverse it. Make your scene come out differently. Does that work? Is it more interesting? If so, use it.
- Pick a moment anywhere in your story. What's your protagonist doing? Try alternatives: What wouldn't your protagonist do right now? What shouldn't she do? What does she secretly want to do? What is she burning to do? Do it.
- Look at anything that happens in your manuscript, any event. Assume your reader saw this coming. What would blow your reader's mind? Great. Do that instead.

EMOTIONAL

- Select a strong event in your story. What's the emotional impact on your protagonist? Work backward to make your protagonist fight that feeling. What can your protagonist do to delay, avoid, or counteract it? Add that.
- Pick a scene. What do you want the reader to feel here? Evoke that emotion through actions alone. Delete all exposition.
- Find a quiet emotional moment. Is it artfully written, delicate, subtle, nuanced, and precise? Congrats. Make it enormous: a tidal wave, an attack, a life-altering earthquake.
- Find an enormous emotional shock. Is it neon, explosive, blistering, painful, and huge? Nice. Underplay it. Instead use irony, throw-away action, or a secondary emotion.

- Pick a point at which your protagonist feels something that everyone feels: love, fear, grief, etc. In this moment, why is your protagonist's experience of this emotion unlike anyone else's? Detail that. Add.

REVEALING AND CHANGING

- Choose any scene. What's your POV character's strongest emotion? Evoke it through actions alone.
- Same scene, using that action: Reverse, rehearse, or otherwise foreshadow the action earlier in the scene, or earlier in the story.
- Same scene: How is your POV character different at the end of the scene than she was at the beginning? How will we know? How will someone else in the scene see it without being told?
- Same scene: What's the biggest thing your POV character does? Is it something small? Make it big, dramatic, or completely outrageous. Is it something big? Make it small, understated, or the opposite of what you first wrote.
- Open your manuscript at random. What's your protagonist's or POV character's secret desire right now? What's inappropriate, a bad idea, or just wrong? Is it more interesting than what you've got? Go there. Do it.
- Open to another random page. What does your protagonist or POV character not want to admit, acknowledge, or face right now? Force it on him.
- Open to another random page. Don't think. Let your protagonist or POV character do whatever she wants to do right now. It's allowed. Good. Now, what does it mean? What is it that your character is suppressing? Enact it, or have your character wish that she could.
- Pick a point when your protagonist is suffering or stuck. Tape her mouth shut. She has to act it out. What does she do?
- Pick a spot where your protagonist is acting out. Put a scolding angel on his shoulder. What does the angel say he should do instead?

Have your protagonist realize the right thing to do, but nevertheless do what's wrong.

- Choose another random spot. Take a quick look; now take a walk. Breathe. Be honest. What are you avoiding? What do you not want to hear? What would your best friend tell you right now, for your own good? Is the same true for your POV character at this moment in the story? Who can say that to him?

HIERARCHY OF EXTERNALIZATION

- Find a point where your protagonist has reactive feelings. Turn them into an action.
- Run through every scene in your manuscript. For each one, write down how circumstances change. Good. That's how your story is advancing, step by step. Is that clear in each scene? Make it clear.
- For each scene note the observable action, what readers will expect, and what's discovered that's new. If actions are lacking, add more. If the expected happens, change it. If nothing new is discovered, discover it and add it.

TURNS AND TWISTS

- Go anywhere in your manuscript. What would blow the story sideways right now? Go for it.
- Find a point at which your protagonist strongly wants to do something. Erect a roadblock. Make it impossible to do.
- Find a point at which your protagonist is blocked. There's a secret door that only you can see. Open it. Go through.
- Pick a character. What's something this character wouldn't do? Do it.
- Pick anything that any character does to advance the story. Assign that action to a different character. Does that work? Use it.

SECRETS

- What secret is your protagonist keeping from the reader? List all clues. Delete all that are obvious. Create three that mislead. Add.
- What's the secret that someone else is keeping from your protagonist? Delete all clues that are obvious. Create three that mislead. Add.
- What's your protagonist keeping from himself, and who sees that before your protagonist does?
- A secret: What's the latest point in the story you can reveal it? When will it inflict maximum damage, or change things the most? Delay until then.

COMEBACK AND REDEMPTION

- What's your protagonist's biggest mistake? What's the worst consequence? Work backwards to build your protagonist's commitment never to make this mistake.
- When your protagonist screws up, who is most let down? Work backwards to make that character's high regard of your protagonist important to both of them.
- When he screws up, what principle does your protagonist violate? Make that principle a foundation of his moral code.
- What's the biggest thing your protagonist must do to make up for her mistake? Work backwards to make this something that your protagonist finds impossible to do.
- Plant the redemptive action earlier. Have others do it, or fail to do it. Make it matter to someone. Build up its symbolic value.

ENDINGS

- What's the big thing your protagonist must do at the end? Make it the one thing your protagonist has sworn never to do.

- What's the place your protagonist must enter at the end? Earlier, make it a place of fear.
- What sacrifice cannot be avoided? Whatever will be sacrificed, make it something your protagonist would never let go.
- What does it mean, in this story, to die? Have your protagonist suffer that death.
- What's the worst thing that could happen to your protagonist? Do it. Go there. Take something away, permanently. Deliver the fear. Enact defeat. Wreck everything. Then find the way back.
- At the end, what's an outcome sweeter than anyone could have imagined? Add it.

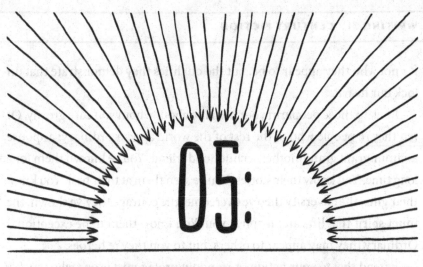

05: STANDOUT CHARACTERS

PROTAGONISTS

Standout main characters are the tent poles that hold up high-impact fiction. Without protagonists who captivate readers there will be, I promise, few readers. So what is it that makes a standout?

It isn't about a protagonist with whom readers can identify. A protagonist with our job, our house, and our headaches isn't an automatic grabber. We may see ourselves in an Everyman or Everywoman, but so what? That doesn't mean we'll care, or at any rate care enough to ride along for hundreds of pages down a painfully familiar road.

Nor are standout characters built of heroic muscle or dark allure. Action heroes and paranormal outsiders are popular, no question, but if unwavering fortitude or suffering sexiness were all that it took, then every action hero and tormented paranormal would be a best-seller. They're not. That's because it's not a protagonist's profile that causes us to care.

It's not who they appear to be, but the qualities they demonstrate that unlock our hearts.

Look to those people in your own life about whom you care greatly. Often they're people who to the rest of the world appear ordinary: a spouse, an immigrant grandmother, a childhood friend. You've known them for a long time. You know their stories. You've seen them at their best. You know their gifts, the adversity they've overcome, the courage they've shown, the inner spirit that lifts and inspires you. You know them to be exceptional. Ordinary they may appear to others, but to you they're heroes.

Extend that to your fiction. A standout protagonist is one who quickly stirs in your reader high admiration. Note the word *quickly*. In your fiction you don't have the luxury of years to spend while your reader gets to know your main character. A bonding born of admiration needs to occur right away, meaning within a page or two of your protagonist's first appearance in the story.

So, what are the qualities that we need to see in action in order for us to care? Everyman and Everywoman protagonists need to show us a hint of why they're not just like us, but that they're exceptional. We need to see in them something strong and good. In the screenwriting business they call this "save the cat," but a demonstration of admirable qualities can happen in many ways.

Lorrie Moore's short story collection *Birds of America* (1998) put her on the literary map, but it was her novel *A Gate at the Stairs* (2009) that propelled her to best-seller lists and an archive's worth of best-of-the-year lists. It's the coming of age story of Tassie Keltjin, the twenty-year-old daughter of an heirloom potato farmer, a university student in an Upper Midwest state that sounds a lot like Wisconsin. On a term break, Tassie needs money. She applies for babysitting jobs and winds up working for a rich, eccentric, and mysterious couple who are adopting a baby.

Okay, stop. Let's think about this. This is a novel about a naïve babysitter? She's nothing special, has no odd talent or paranormal ability, no back-story drama, nothing? She's utterly ordinary? Yes. So why are we supposed to read about her? Why should we even go beyond the first page? There's no reason at all, but luckily Lorrie Moore knows this and gives us a reason. Look at this chunk of Tassie's opening narrative and see if you can spot it:

> I was looking in December for work that would begin at the start of the January term. I'd finished my exams and was answering ads from the student job board, ones for "childcare provider." I liked children—I did!—or rather, I liked them OK. They were sometimes interesting. I admired their stamina and candor. And I was good with them in that I could make funny faces at the babies and with the older children teach them card tricks and speak in the theatrically sarcastic tones that disarmed and enthralled them. But I was not especially skilled at minding children for long spells; I grew bored, perhaps like my own mother. After I spent too much time playing their games, my mind grew peckish and longed to lose itself in some book I had in my backpack. I was ever hopeful of early bedtimes and long naps.

Time's up. Got it? The reason we immediately care about Tassie Keltjin? Correct. She's funny. It's a pleasure to listen to her. She's got a wonderfully ironic take on things, especially herself. As she tries to convince herself that she'll enjoy babysitting, it's painfully obvious that she won't. Editors like to call this quality "voice," but I think it's more accurate to call it "a narrator we enjoy spending time with." Moore knows her Plain Jane heroine has little to offer, so she endows her a strong and attractive quality: humor. Happily for us, it never lets up.

The paradox of already heroic protagonists is that for all their skill, strength, and unwavering idealism, we still won't necessarily cheer for them. That's because they're too perfect. How can we bond to a paragon when we haven't a prayer of ever measuring up? Instead of making us cheer, they cause us to feel inadequate. What heroic protagonists need to show us is that they're human.

Rick Riordan's massively successful *Percy Jackson & the Olympians* series not only has been #1 on the *New York Times* Best Sellers List, but also has won more awards and accolades then you can shake a lightning bolt at. It's about Percy Jackson, a kid who is the half-breed child of one of the old Greek gods, Poseidon. He's had to battle all kinds of mythological monsters and the nasty Titans. At the opening of the fifth book in the series, *The Last Olympian* (2009), Percy and his half-blood friends are gearing up for a final battle (in Manhattan) against the Titan lord Kronos. Percy's a true hero, but Rick Riordan knows he must also make him a kid, which he does in the novel's opening lines:

> The end of the world started when a pegasus landed on the hood of my car.
>
> Up until then, I was having a great afternoon. Technically I wasn't supposed to be driving because I wouldn't turn sixteen for another week, but my mom and stepdad, Paul, took my friend Rachel and me to this private stretch of beach on the South Shore, and Paul let us borrow his Prius for a short spin.
>
> Now, I know what you're thinking, *Wow, that was really irresponsible of him, blah, blah, blah,* but Paul knows me pretty well. He's seen me slice up demons and leap out of exploding school buildings, so he probably figured taking a car a few hundred yards wasn't exactly the most dangerous thing I'd ever done.
>
> Anyway, Rachel and I were driving along. It was a hot August day. Rachel's red hair was pulled back in a ponytail and she wore a white blouse over her swimsuit. I'd never seen her in anything but ratty T-shirts and paint-splattered jeans before, and she looked like a million golden drachma.

Percy is learning to drive and crushing on his suddenly hot-looking friend Rachel. Pretty normal, wouldn't you say? That's the point. That Percy is just like any almost-sixteen-year-old means that Riordan's young readers will have no problem bonding with him.

Dark protagonists have the toughest challenge of all: to promise us that the torment they endure will be worth it; that not only is there redemption waiting down the road, but that they desire it. No one wants to live with someone else's unrelenting suffering. It's just so hopeless. But when there's a glimmer of hope, we're drawn in. When change becomes possible, it becomes okay to care.

If a young adult novel nowadays involves death, suffering, struggle, eternity, remorse, a tormented paranormal male, and a clueless human female, you can count on one thing: romance. It might seem impossible for any author to break through the wall of popularity erected by Stephenie Meyer's *Twilight* series, but Lauren Kate's *Fallen* series did so. It's about seventeen-year-old Lucinda "Luce" Price, who at a reform school meets brooding Daniel Grigori, whom we learn is a fallen angel and her forever boyfriend. The problem is they keep meeting over and over again through time. When she's seventeen he kisses her, she dies, and they start all over again—except that Luce never remembers the past and Daniel does. In the series opener, *Fallen* (2009), Daniel kisses Luce and she doesn't die. Something is different this time.

The second volume, *Torment* (2010), opens with Daniel beset with worries unique to a fallen angel with a girlfriend whose existence hinges on a (as yet unexplained) cosmic struggle. There's an eighteen-day truce on, during which many will try to kill Luce, including Miss Sophia and her cohorts, the Twenty-four Elders of Zhsmaelin, not to mention the Outcasts, who are sort of nasty freelance angels shunned by both Heaven and Hell. A temporary hope is that Luce will be safe at a special school for Nephilim on the California coast. Poor Daniel. The kid's got a lot on his mind. What with his girlfriend cursed to die every time she turns seventeen, you could say he's tormented. Who wouldn't be depressed?

Except who wants to read about a depressed protagonist? No one, really, so Lauren Kate makes sure that her readers have an immediate reason to bond with suffering Daniel. Her opening finds him on a beach near Sausalito with series regular Cam, who is crouched over the corpse of an Outcast whom they have just killed:

> Daniel stared out at the bay. His eyes were gray as the thick fog enveloping the Sausalito shoreline, as the choppy water lapping the pebble beach beneath his feet. There was no violet to his eyes now at all; he could feel it. She was too far away.
>
> He braced himself against the biting gale off the water. But even as he tugged his thick black pea coat closer, he knew it was no use. Hunting always left him cold.
>
> Only one thing could warm him today, and she was out of reach. He missed the way the crown of her head made the perfect resting spot for his lips. He imagined filling the circle of his arms with her body, leaning down to kiss her neck. But it was a good thing Luce couldn't be here now. What she'd see would horrify her.

What is it that makes Daniel someone to care about, apart from his awesome J. Crew pea coat? Right, he's in love. More, while he misses his girl, he also longs to protect her from ugly realities she doesn't yet know. His thoughts are romantic: he misses kissing and hugging. No alpha male lust for this angel. After his girlfriend dies the first dozen times, he could be forgiven for, you know, finding another girlfriend, but Luce is the one. He's loyal. For sure, he just slaughtered an Outcast, but, hey, underneath he's really sweet. All this is conveyed in the novel's opening three paragraphs. Lauren Kate makes sure we have reasons to care.

Have you ever read a published novel only to find yourself feeling indifferent about the character whose journey you're being asked to take? If so, then you see what I mean. Emotional bonding doesn't come from sympathy, perfection, or fantasy fulfillment, but from feeling that a character is worthy of our devotion.

When protagonists quickly earn your heart, then you are emotionally bonded instead of bluntly indifferent. That's the effect you want to have on your readers, isn't it? Good. Next comes making sure that your main character's grip on the reader doesn't relax.

LIVING TOGETHER

After falling in love comes a brief honeymoon. Then all too soon begins the more difficult business of learning to live together. It's the same with readers and your protagonist. Bonding can't be taken for granted. The good qualities that made it possible to fall in love in the first place need reinforcement.

Unfortunately, many fiction writers fall back on looks and charm, or rather their literary equivalents: quirks and special abilities. Not that there's anything necessarily wrong with those.

Quirks are the easiest distinction to pin on protagonists. They're a staple of detective fiction. From Holmes's addiction to morphine to Dexter's proclivity for killing serial killers, quirks have always made characters more interesting. But what is a quirk as opposed to a character trait? What makes quirks fascinating?

Let's say I like the color blue. Nothing special in that. Let's suppose I'm obsessed: live in blue rooms, drive a blue car, and wear only blue shirts. Maybe I collect indigo dyes and Delftware pottery. A bit strange, okay, but it's still barely worth noting. Now, suppose my name is "Red." Suppose I'm a detective in the red clay state of Georgia. Maybe my father was a pro baseball player who pitched a season for the Boston Red Sox, hence my name. Now my obsession with blue becomes a bit strange. It begs questions. It's effective because inherent in it is a contradiction.

Markus Zusak's *The Book Thief* (2005) is a holocaust story that was a #1 *New York Times* best-seller and won a ridiculous number of awards and accolades. Set in Germany in 1939, it's about a girl, Liesel Meminger, who pulls from the snow a book, *The Grave Digger's Handbook*, which starts her on a life of crime with a peculiar focus: she steals books. She steals them from

Nazi bonfires, the library of the mayor's wife, anywhere she can get them. But Zusak builds into this scenario a huge contradiction: Liesel cannot read.

Oh. Huh? Why does an illiterate girl care enough about books to steal them? Well, that's the point. That puzzle keeps us hooked. As Liesel learns to read with her foster-father's loving help, and they face peril by hiding a Jew in their basement, the purpose of this contradiction comes clear: It's a multifold metaphor for the spirit of freedom and a thirst for understanding that cannot be burned away. Books represent all that's good.

Special abilities have long been a novelist's stock in trade. Once limited to science fiction and fantasy, bookstore shelves today abound with characters who possess magical powers, paranormal gifts, and exotic handicaps.

Sarah Addison Allen's best-selling debut novel, *Garden Spells* (2007), is built around a small-town North Carolina family, the Waverleys, who have a garden's worth of odd gifts. In fact, the family garden is itself magical, its herbs and fruits aiding in everything from keeping secrets to seeing in the dark. (Most special of all is the apple tree: an apple from its branches, when eaten, will show one's future. Amusingly, the tree is in the habit of throwing apples at people whom it wants to change.) The novel's heroine is Claire, a caterer whose success has much to do with the salubrious (sometimes erotic) qualities of her dishes. Her Aunt Evanelle also has a strange gift: the urge to stockpile unneeded items, such as toasters and pants, which later prove to be prescient gifts for neighbors: exactly the right thing at exactly the time they need it.

The magical qualities of the Waverleys and their garden are more than just a charming Southern magical realism overlay. They become a metaphor for the healing power of family connections. Claire especially needs this healing when her comfortably routine life is upended by the return to town of her gypsy sister, Sydney, fleeing an abusive relationship, and Sydney's daughter, Bay. Old resentment runs deep between the sisters, and erupts without warning:

"There's a reason I am the way I am, you know," Claire blurted out, because she had to explain it to someone.

Sydney grabbed a can of Coke and turned to her curiously.

"We didn't have a home, Mom and I, the first six years of my life. We slept in cars and homeless shelters. She did a lot of stealing, and a lot of sleeping around. You never knew that, did you?" Claire asked. Sydney had the Coke can halfway to her mouth, frozen. She slowly shook her head and lowered the can. "Sometimes I got the feeling you romanticized what her life was like before she came back to Bascom. I don't know if she ever intended to stay, but when we came here, I knew I was never going to leave. The house and Grandma Waverley were permanent things, and when I was young, that's all I ever dreamed of. But then you were born, and I was so jealous of you. You were given that security from the moment you entered the world. It's my fault, our relationship as kids. I made it contentious because you were from here and I wasn't. I'm sorry. I'm sorry I'm not good at being a sister. I'm sorry I'm not good with Tyler. I know you want me to be. But I can't seem to help it. I can't help but think how temporary everything is, and I'm scared of that kind of temporary. I'm scared of people leaving me."

Claire's all-too-human desire for security and safety is understandable. It would be enough of a wound around which to build a novel of hometown healing; indeed, Claire's problems are pretty routine in the world of women's fiction. What makes her story special is that she's a witch, of sorts, who's unable to cast spells for herself. Her balm needs a different catalyst: love, especially the love of her sister, her last connection to her past.

Special abilities work best when they're intrinsic to the action; that is, the story couldn't happen without them. In the case of *Garden Spells*, the apple tree does play a critical part in saving Sydney from her abusive partner, who tracks her down, but the more essential role of the Waverley's special abilities is to show, by their insufficiency, that making things right in one's life takes more than magic: It calls for the greater ability to love.

There are some other novelistic tricks for keeping protagonists interesting. Unexpected actions are a muscular technique for lifting main characters above their peers. It's not hard to see the reason for that. Unexpected actions make us wonder *why?* They intrigue. They puzzle. They snap us awake. We think, "Excuse me?" and then of course we have to read on for further illumination.

Secondary characters are a good opportunity to work on this, too. Mostly they act as we expect, but an out-of-character action can make them memorable. The technique is simple to explain: start with a stereotype and find a way to reverse it.

Pittacus Lore's *New York Times* best-seller *I Am Number Four* (2010) is a young adult novel about an alien teenager hiding on Earth. He's one of nine surviving kids from the doomed planet Lorien. The kids are the remnants of an elite called the Garde, who as adolescents develop multiple powers called Legacies. They're hiding from a vile enemy race named the Mogadorians, who are out to kill them. Due to a charm placed upon the Garde youngsters, though, the Mogadorians must kill them in numerical order.

As Lore's novel opens, the third Lorien kid has been killed. The novel's hero is number four. He knows he's next. Currently known as John Smith, he and his Cêpan (guardian adult) relocate to a rural nowhere ironically named Paradise, Ohio, where John enrolls in high school. The school is typical and the kids there fit the roles John expects to see. There's a jock hero who's a bully. There's a blonde cheerleader. There's a geek best friend. Happily, Lore plays with their stereotypes. The blonde cheerleader has had an awakening, and has given up cheerleading for photography and work at a wild animal refuge. The jock bully proves to be a stand-up guy. But what of the geek best friend?

In this book he's named Sam Goode, a pretty typical geek except that he's geekier and odder than usual. He wears thick glasses that he doesn't need. (They're his missing father's glasses; he wears them thinking he'll be able to see what his dad sees.) He also believes in alien abductions, and subscribes to a paranoid aliens-are-among-us magazine. When he begins to suspect that John is actually an alien, how do you think this geek reacts? He might say *cool!* He might be awed by John's super powers. He might want to know everything about life on another planet. But that's not how Sam Goode reacts. Instead, he's terrified. When John shows up unexpectedly at his house, Sam pulls a gun:

> "Whoa," I say, instinctively lifting my hands in front of me. "What's going on?"
>
> He stands up. His hands are shaking. The gun is pointed at my chest. I think that he's lost his mind.
>
> "Tell me what you are," he says.
>
> "What are you talking about?"
>
> "I saw what you did in those woods. You're not human." I was afraid of this, that he saw more than I had hoped.
>
> "This is crazy, Sam! I got into a fight. I've been doing martial arts for years."
>
> "Your hands lit up like flashlights. You could throw people around like they were nothing. That's not normal."
>
> …
>
> I roll my eyes. "Yes, I'm an alien, Sam. I'm from a planet hundreds of millions of miles away. I have superpowers. Is that what you want to hear?"
>
> He stares at me, his hands still shaking.
>
> "Do you realize how stupid that sounds? Quit being crazy and put the gun down."

How often does a geek pull a gun? That's my point. It runs against type (heck, how does a geek get a gun to begin with?), and therefore is a surprise. Is there a character in your novel who can counter our expectations? Pick one. What's one thing she would never do? Bingo. When she does it, we'll be snapped awake.

Even stronger than surprise is selfless focus. Main characters who care about others are highly admirable. Selfless concern melts our hearts and warms us to characters as surely as sunshine melts ice or as surely as the loyal gaze of a pet dog's big brown eyes.

Indeed, it's the selfless devotion of a dog, Enzo, that immediately endears us to this point-of-view creature in Garth Stein's longtime best-seller *The Art of Racing in the Rain* (2008). Enzo's human owner is an aspiring racecar driver, Denny, whose talent is subverted by the necessities of life in Seattle: making a living, marriage, parenthood. As the novel opens, Denny is alone and floundering in his job behind the service counter at a car dealership. Enzo has grown old. He wants to die. One evening he urinates on the floor and waits for Denny to come home. It's part of a plan to show Denny that it's time for him to make his final trip to the vet, but Denny misunderstands:

> He says, "Sorry I was late. I should have come straight home, but the guys from work insisted. I told Craig I was quitting, and . . ."
>
> He trails off, and I realize that he thinks that my accident was because he was *late*. Oh, no. That's not how it was meant. It's so hard to communicate because there are so many moving parts. There's presentation and there's interpretation and they're so dependent on each other it makes things very difficult. I didn't want him to feel bad about this. I wanted him to see the obvious, that's it's okay for him to let me go. He's been going through so much, and he's finally through it. He needs to not have me around to worry about anymore. He needs me to free him to be brilliant.

Talk about self-sacrifice! An elderly dog who wants to die so his owner can be free to shine? If at this point in Stein's opening you are not mentally thinking *Awwwwww . . .* well, then you are made of stone. Or you're a cat person. Regardless, you have to admit that Stein has found a narrator with nearly irresistible selfless focus.

What could be better than selflessness? Serene perspective. Rising above it all, adopting the mountaintop view, showing maturity: There are

plenty of ways to put it, but the essential technique is to give your protagonist a godlike viewpoint.

Earlier in this chapter I mentioned Lorrie Moore's *A Gate at the Stairs*,
about a naïve university student and babysitter whose strength is her humor. Did I make it sound like little happens in this novel? Compared to
some commercial fiction, little does. But Moore's novel is not devoid of
drama. Her narrator's awakening flows from the revelation of the secrets
kept by her lover, a veteran of the war in Afghanistan, and the couple for
whom she babysits. Both are tragic stories, yet Tassie's narrative voice is
comic. Moore thus faces the tough problem of reconciling these conflicting modes. How are we supposed to laugh when what's happened to her
characters is so sad?

It's a storyteller's dilemma. Moore solves it by making her heroine,
Tassie, aware of this very problem, as we see after the truth has surfaced:

> Tragedies, I was coming to realize through my daily studies in the
> humanities both in and out of the classroom, were a luxury. They
> were constructions of an affluent society, full of sorrow and truth
> but without moral function . . . The weakening of the soul, the story
> of downfall and failed overcoming—trains missed, letters not re-
> ceived, pride flaring, the demolition of one's own offspring, who
> were then served up in stews—this was awe-inspiring, wounding
> entertainment told uselessly and in comfort at tables full of love and
> money. Where life was meagerer, where the tables were only half
> full, the comic triumph of the poor was the useful demi-lie. Jokes
> were needed. *And then the baby fell down the stairs.* This could be
> funny! . . . And to ease the suffering of the listener, things had better
> be funny. Though they weren't always. And his is how, sometimes,
> stories failed us: Not that funny. Or worse, not funny in the least.

Tassie's meditation on the moral responsibility of stories, and their failure
sometimes to do the tranquilizing job of being funny, is pretty sophisticated
for a potato farmer's daughter. But that's the point. Moore allows her main

character's wit to coexist with terrible events, and on top of that gives her the authority of a moral philosopher. Tassie is entertaining but has even more than that to offer us. She rewards our attention with her serene perspective.

All of those techniques are effective in building protagonists who appeal to readers, but intriguing readers isn't the same as keeping them emotionally hooked. Looks and charm will only get you so far. Readers' devotion to main characters is earned, page after page, through their actions. Strength and goodness won your readers' hearts in the first place. It's also what will keep the flame burning.

By all means, give your main characters standout qualities. Follow the hierarchy of effectiveness: quirks, special abilities, unexpected actions, selfless focus, and serene perspective. Use them all and you'll have fascinating main characters.

THE GOOD IN THE BAD

In the world of fiction there's a misunderstood minority who desperately need our study, understanding, and compassion: antagonists.

Villains are constantly vilified. They're portrayed in stereotypes. It's so unfair! I mean, aren't they human beings (usually) just like you and me? They deserve better. They need a bill of rights: the right to be portrayed realistically, to receive a fair hearing, to equal page time opportunity, to freedom of belief. Honestly, they should organize a march. Their treatment in the pages of manuscripts is a community-wide shame.

Who is the principle antagonist in your current work in progress? If you have a villain as such, the answer is easy. If you don't—or if your villain is hidden, as in a mystery novel—identify the character who most opposes, drags down, works against, and throws doubt upon your protagonist. That's your antagonist.

How is this character portrayed? In most manuscripts, antagonists are two-dimensional stereotypes. How is this character motivated? Usually antagonist motivation is simple, single, and purely malevolent. How busy is this antagonist? Not very, I'll bet. Villains mostly are employed part time, popping into the story once in a while to rub their hands and let out an evil chuckle. What sort of relationship does your antagonist have with your protagonist? Usually they're distant; sometimes they're not even acquainted. The results are characters who fail to come alive, feel real, or even scare. Being predictable has that effect.

Effective antagonists receive as much planning and work as other characters. To make them real you've got to get into them, like them, and maybe even love them. How else will they thrive? Extending compassion, care, and understanding to your antagonist isn't necessarily easy, I'll admit, but it's your responsibility. To make it easier, think of finding the good in your baddie. If you do, then the awful things they do will be doubly dramatic.

Suzanne Collins's massive young adult best-seller *The Hunger Games* (2008) is the story of Katniss Everdeen, who lives in a horrible future America. Following a devastating collapse, her new world of Panem is ruled from a remote city called the Capitol west of what once were known as the Rocky Mountains. Katniss lives in District 12, where coal is mined but little is given in return. Hunger is a way of life. Overshadowing all is the annual subjugation known as the Hunger Games. As punishment for a failed rebellion, every year two children from each district, one boy and one girl, are chosen by random lottery to participate in a televised event in which they fight to the death. One winner emerges, earning for their district an extra, but still meager, food ration.

When Katniss's delicate twelve-year-old sister is improbably selected as a District 12 "tribute," Katniss, a skilled bow hunter, volunteers to take her place. Her fight for survival in the Hunger Games is a brutal ordeal whose antagonists, the other tributes, are obvious. But Suzanne Collins has a problem. Her story is about children killing children. Even though they have no choice, it's a morally repugnant situation. One solution would be to portray the other tributes as monsters, but the true enemy is the government of Panem; however, for the purposes of this volume in her trilogy, that government needs to remain remote and all-powerful.

Collins tackles this novelistic challenge in a skillful way. Rather than demonizing the other tributes, she humanizes them, even the "Careers" who are strong, well fed, and trained for the Hunger Games. (One of them even spares Katniss because she staged a moving funeral for the other tribute from his district.) Instead, Collins constructs two other antagonists for Katniss. They're more interesting because they ostensibly are on her side. One is the boy tribute from District 12, a baker's son named Peeta, who may or may not be in love with her. The other is District 12's only other surviving tribute, a now-middle-aged drunk named Haymitch. Unfortunately, Haymitch is to briefly train Katniss and Peeta before the game begins. He can help them during the game, too, by lining up sponsors who send in supplies.

But Haymitch hates Katniss, so she thinks. She certainly doesn't like him. His advice for survival is scant: "Stay alive." But early in the novel there's a hint that Katniss and Peeta may have won his respect. He trains them and guides them effectively through the pre-game publicity events. During the game he parachutes in supplies, even managing to send messages of encouragement with their timing. Toward the novel's end, Katniss gains insight into Haymitch when she and Peeta speculate on how this physically unimpressive man, later a lonely drunk, once won the game:

> "He outsmarted the others," says Peeta.
>
> I nod, then let the conversation drop. But secretly I'm wondering if Haymitch sobered up long enough to help Peeta and me because he thought we just might have the wits to survive. Maybe he wasn't always a drunk. Maybe, in the beginning, he tried to help the tributes. But then it got unbearable. It must be hell to mentor kids and then watch them die. Year after year after year. I realize that if I get out of here, that will become my job. To mentor the girl from District 12. The idea is so repellent, I thrust it from my mind.

Collins thus justifies the decrepit drunk Haymitch. She makes him understandable to the reader by redeeming him for Katniss. He has a reason for being the way he is. He has a relationship with Katniss and plenty to do, as well, even if he's physically off stage.

When pure evildoers do evil, we simply shrug. When three-dimensional human beings for whom we have feelings do something wrong, we're deeply disturbed. That's because we've taken them inside. Their wrongdoing becomes something we ourselves might have done. And that's scary. Your main objective in creating antagonists, then, is not just to generate opposition for your protagonist, but to hold up a mirror to your reader— or maybe to yourself.

Making an antagonist real may not be wholly comfortable. But that's the storyteller's job: to look inside, take what you find, and transform it. None of us are entirely bad or utterly good. We're forgiving of ourselves, though. Why not extend that understanding to antagonists? Or simply look at it this way: What will make your antagonists memorable isn't the evil that they do, but the good.

SECONDARY CHARACTERS

Secondary characters can be colorless tagalongs, but they also can be the most vibrant people on the page. But even when they are sharply drawn they can be simplistic, in effect their own stereotype.

To make secondary characters fully rounded, they need to be as three-dimensional, conflicted, and changing as your main character. One of the most dynamic measures of a secondary character's genuineness is his changing relationship to your main character. When effective, none of that is faked. Such characters are best when they're not what we expect and their actions surprise us.

The top standout secondary character in contemporary fiction has got to be Lisbeth Salander, the titular character of Stieg Larsson's *The Girl With the*

Dragon Tattoo (2005). In the hands of another writer, she would be a miserable victim. A violent and promiscuous problem child, a veteran of foster homes, she is described in her casebook "with terms such as *introverted, socially inhibited, lacking in empathy, ego-fixated, psychopathic and asocial behavior, difficulty in cooperating,* and *incapable of assimilating learning.*"

Lisbeth has for twelve years been under the social and psychiatric guardianship of the state, her assets controlled by a court-appointed trustee. You'd think she'd be a failure on the margins of society, but she's far from that. She works as an investigator for a security firm. Her research is devastatingly accurate and impeccably documented. That's because she's a hacker, one of the best in the world and secretly connected to her shadowy peers. She begins the novel investigating its overt protagonist, the unfairly disgraced financial journalist Mikael Blomkvist, but later becomes his ally, his lover, and eventually his savior.

Lisbeth is about as distinctive as secondary characters get. She's tattooed, secretive, suspicious, and contemptuous of others. She respects no one's boundaries but fiercely protects her own. She's a cipher who is strangely driven to uncover every secret of the people in her path. She lives outside the law yet has a fierce sense of justice. Her apartment looks like a bomb went off in it, but mentally she's highly organized. She's a collection of conflicting sides, and these contradictions make her fascinating.

All this would be good enough for Lisbeth to fulfill her role in the story. But Stieg Larsson doesn't stop there. The story sends Mikael Blomkvist on a year-long hiatus from the financial journal he founded (three of those months are spent in a low-security prison), during which he is hired to investigate the decades-old disappearance of a girl, Harriet Vanger, a member of one of Sweden's most wealthy families. Lisbeth aids Blomkvist. A relationship develops. It's different than any Lisbeth has experienced:

> When Salander went to bed on her seventh night in Hedeby, she
> was mildly irritated with Blomkvist. For almost a week she had

spent practically every waking minute with him. Normally seven minutes of another person's company was enough to give her a headache, so she set things up to live as a recluse. She was perfectly content as long as people left her in peace. Unfortunately society was not very smart or understanding; she had to protect herself from social authorities, child welfare authorities, guardianship authorities, tax authorities, police, curators, psychologists, psychiatrists, teachers, and bouncers, who (apart from the guys watching the door at Kvarnen, who by this time knew who she was) would never let her into the bar even though she was twenty-five. There was a whole army of people who seemed not to have anything better to do than to try to disrupt her life, and, if they were given the opportunity, to correct the way she had chosen to live it.

It did no good to cry, she had learned that early on. She had also learned that every time she tried to make someone aware of something in her life, the situation just got worse. Consequently, it was up to her to solve her problems by herself, using whatever methods she deemed necessary. Something that Advokat Bjurman [*see the novel*] had found out the hard way.

Blomkvist had the same tiresome habit as everyone else, poking around in her life and asking questions. On the other hand, he did not react at all like most other men she had met.

When she ignored his questions he simply shrugged and left her in peace. Astounding.

Will her relationship with Blomkvist change Lisbeth? Although she saves his life and even vindicates him in the case of the journalistic defamation that sent him to prison, Larsson leaves the issue unresolved until the very end, when Lisbeth finally has a revelation:

What she had realized was that love was the moment when your heart was about to burst.

Lisbeth decides to tell Blomkvist how she feels, but, alas, is foiled at the last moment. Further development of their relationship is made to wait for the following volumes of Larsson's trilogy, but the more important fact is that Lisbeth has changed . . . or rather, has been changed by her relationship with Blomkvist. That this most asocial of secondary characters can open herself to someone else is what makes her, finally, a true standout.

Lisbeth Salander's relationship to Mikael Blomkvist builds as *The Girl With the Dragon Tattoo* progresses. However, it's also possible to drive in the other direction: to establish a strong relationship between protagonist and secondary, then mess it up. That pattern provides a lot of extra drama in Michael Koryta's *The Cypress House* (2011), one of the eerie and highly successful stand-alone thrillers that Koryta began to produce after developing his chops in his Lincoln Perry detective series.

Set in the Depression, *The Cypress House* is about an itinerant laborer, Arlen Wagner, who has inherited an awful special ability: When someone will soon die, he sees smoke swirling in her eye sockets. As the novel opens, Arlen is aboard a train full of Veterans Work Program workers bound for camps in the Florida Keys. At a stop along the way in northern Florida he sees smoke in the eyes of all of his fellow passengers. They've got to leave the train. But of course no one believes him. Only his traveling companion, a nineteen-year-old mechanical genius named Paul Brickhill, to whom Arlen has become a father figure, disembarks with him.

Stranded in rural Florida, Arlen and Paul hitch a ride and wind up at an inn that has suspiciously few visitors, called The Cypress House, run by a tight-lipped beauty named Rebecca Cady. The area in which they've landed, Corridor County, is highly corrupt. The inlet on which The Cypress House sits is a transit site for heroin smuggled from Cuba. The Cypress House itself is where the money is counted, by Rebecca, and brutal enforcement is done.

The two men set about fixing up Rebecca's place, Paul reconstructing a generator with wizardly skill. Paul also falls in love with Rebecca. That's unfortunate, because Arlen can see smoke in Paul's eyes when Paul shakes hands with corrupt judge and crime kingpin Solomon Wade. Paul will *die* here. He must leave. But how can Arlen convince him to go? He can't. He can only drive Paul away, which he does by himself sleeping with Rebecca—and making sure that Paul knows. Sure enough, Paul storms away.

The relationship between the two men is apparently destroyed. Meanwhile, Arlen learns Rebecca's back-story, why she is trapped in Corridor County, and her nearly hopeless plan for escaping from Solomon Wade. Arlen determines to help her, even though toward the end he looks in a rear view mirror and sees smoke in his own eyes.

Now, let me ask you: Is Paul Brickhill really necessary to the story? Strictly speaking, no. Arlen and Rebecca's escape from Corridor County could have been perfectly well played out by just the two of them. So why does Koryta include Paul? For a couple of reasons. Arlen's mentoring of Paul makes him a big degree warmer, which is important as Koryta's temperature as a stylist is cool (see chapter eight). Paul also returns just before the novel's violent climax. He's kidnapped by the bad guys, giving Arlen additional stakes and a more urgent reason to kill Solomon Wade.

Arlen's devotion to Paul is extra poignant, not only because of their shared history but because the father-son trust between them is, of necessity, shattered earlier in the story. We want them to reconcile. And happily they do, much later, in the novel's resolution pages:

> They finished their Coca-Colas and then Paul's train was boarding, and they got to their feet. Arlen wanted to help him with his bags but he didn't yet have the strength.
>
> "You're going to her, aren't you?" Paul said. It was the first either of them had spoken directly of Rebecca.
>
> "Yes," Arlen said.
>
> Paul looked away, managed a faint smile, and said, "You tell her I said hello. Please?"
>
> "I will. You know that. And I love her, Paul. I hope you understand that."

Paul nodded. "Yeah. Didn't make me glad at first, doesn't really now, but maybe there'll come a day . . . anyhow, I know you do. I know it, and it matters."

It doesn't matter who a secondary character is or what role they take in the story. Distinctive characters are a plus, without a doubt, but even plain vanilla pals can spring off the page when they are conflicted and engaged in dynamic, unfolding relationships with others.

WARM AND ALIVE

There are two ways to feel about people: warmly or coolly. That's true of you and your characters too. You feel one way or the other about them. Probably you love your protagonist, or think you do, but that doesn't always come across on the page. It's the same with secondary characters. You can tell when an author's got ambivalent feelings. Those characters come across as dull, or perhaps they don't come alive at all. They're like place holders.

Working up warmth about every character you portray is a lot of work, no question, but remember you're asking hundreds of thousands of readers to be interested, if not fascinated, by the people in your story. How can you accomplish that if you aren't yourself fascinated first?

What is it that makes a person deeply fascinating to you? Knowledge? Mystery? Complexity? Command? Everyone's answer is likely different, but I suspect there's one quality that universally makes others absorbing to us: passionate engagement in life.

Awake, aware, discerning, curious, compassionate, gripped, immersed . . . we could define this quality in any number of ways. We can also see it for what it isn't: aloof, cold, hard, apathetic, cynical, unfeeling, detached. To put it another way, we're put off by people who are downers but attracted to people who are vitally alive.

That's odd, considering how often protagonists in manuscripts are supreme downers. How are we supposed to engage—and stay engaged for hundreds of pages—with characters who are dead inside? Now, that is not to say that our heroes and heroines shouldn't ever feel low, discouraged, or even defeated. That's natural and can be dramatic. But there's a difference between feeling something negative and not caring about it. Apathy is an awful burden for you, your characters, and your readers. Few will tolerate it for long.

Any unhappy inclination or mood can be portrayed on the page. What will either push us away or draw us deeper in is how it's handled. Is the negative feeling unrelentingly awful, or is it something that holds some interest for the one suffering it? Any black feeling is palatable if it's a puzzle. Torment is an opportunity for study.

Even just a degree of objectivity can ease the sting of a painful inner state. Jennifer Donnelly's highly praised second novel, *Revolution* (2010), tackles one of the most difficult of all formats, the past-present story (see chapter six). In this case there isn't even a link between eras. There's no time travel, no family connection, no secret that demands to be unearthed, and no academic mystery to be solved. Nothing. There's only a contemporary Brooklyn teenager on the edge, Andi Alpers, whose life is barely holding together. In the past, discovered through a diary, is a girl who lived through and beyond the French Revolution, Alexandrine Paradis, a thwarted actress who became the mysterious Green Man, a pyrotechnical terrorist whose fireworks displays lit the skies of Revolutionary-era Paris.

On a winter break in Paris with her father, Andi comes across Alexandrine's diary. As she reads it, she's caught up in Alexandrine's struggles, her fight for survival, and her devotion to the eight-year-old heir to the French throne, Louis-Charles, who was imprisoned and may have died (or survived), and whose innocent suffering drove Alexandrine mad. Andi identifies with Alexandrine. Gradually the events of the diarist's life mirror, then fuse, with her own. Or perhaps she gains a new perspective on her problems. Regardless, Andi recognizes that she has something to learn, as she sees in recalling something her history teacher said:

Ms. Hammond sighed. "History is a Rorschach test, people," she said. "What you see when you look at it tells you as much about yourself as it does about the past."

I remember Ms. Hammond's words when I think about Alex. She was there. A part of it all. She saw history up close and personal. And what she saw made her insane.

Andi's own hopelessness gradually changes to hope, as she realizes one evening:

I lay my head on my pillow. I'm afraid to read any more.

Please let this have a happy ending. Let one thing in this shitty world have a happy ending.

Jennifer Donnelly seeks to connect past and present when no actual connection exists, except through the palpable need of a troubled American teen to get a grip on her life by reading the story of a girl who lived two hundred years before. She's even aware of this therapeutic process, and it's that objectivity that lifts Andi Alpers above her misery and allows her into our hearts.

Self-examination allows a storm to rage in your character while simultaneously giving shelter to your readers. It's a clinical trick, a psychotherapist's staple. Feel the feeling, but then objectify it. Without denying the feeling, that takes away the sting.

If negativity is a negative, there's a similar danger in sunniness. If downers repel us, you would think that happy characters would attract us. That's true, but only to a point. Characters lacking conflict also lack a story. Plus, optimists are annoying. *Get real*, we think. *Get your head out of the sand!*

Nevertheless, some characters are content. How then do you stir unease in your readers when nothing's wrong? How do you then make such characters interesting? Here's a clue: Candide. Did you suspect that Voltaire's satiric hero wasn't actually living in the best of all possible worlds?

There you go. There is delicious tension in a hint of doubt. Even *sunny days have a few clouds.*

Take a look at Christmas stories, for example. They're a staple in publishers' catalogues. You can find them in many flavors: inspirational, mysterious, and especially romantic. They're harder to pull off than they appear because Christmas is a happy time. Eggnog and good cheer are the antithesis of story, the opposite of conflict. So, how do you create a cloud when everything's jolly?

The reliable and best-selling historical romance author Eloisa James can be counted on for wicked, yet cleverly clean, fun with her endless supply of duchess heroines. In her 2007 holiday offering, *An Affair Before Christmas*, it's Lady Perdita "Poppy" Selby. As the novel opens in Paris at Christmastime, young and inexperienced Poppy has fallen in love with the hot Duke of Fletcher, and he with her. Their first scene is a chaste love fest:

> "It's almost miraculous, how we feel about each other."
>
> Fletch blinked and looked down at his bride-to-be, Miss Perdita Selby. For a moment Notre Dame, Poppy and Christmas were confusingly mixed in his mind: as if a cathedral were more erotic than a woman; as if a woman were more sacred than the holiday.
>
> She smiled up at him, her face framed by soft curls, the color of white gold streaked with sunlight, her mouth as sweet and ripe as any French plum. "You don't think it's too good to be true, Fletch? You don't, do you?"

Look again. It's easy to miss the mild apprehension in that passage. In case you didn't pick it up, James delivers a stronger clue later in the scene when Fletch kisses Poppy:

> "Eeek! What are you doing?"
>
> "Kissing you," he said, dropping his arms from around her shoulders because she was whacking him with her muff and it seemed the right thing to do.

"That is disgusting," she said, glaring at him. "Disgusting! You don't think that duchesses go around doing that kind of thing, do you?"

"Kissing?" he asked helplessly.

"Kissing like *that*. You put your—your saliva in my mouth!"

Uh-oh, trouble ahead. If Poppy's put off by a little spit swapping, how's she going to feel about full-on sex? So it proves to be. Poppy doesn't . . . pop. She's an ice princess on the sheets. Four years later Fletch is desperate, though still in love with her. The remainder of the story drives them apart, but eventually Poppy finds her groove. The affair of the title isn't with a lover, of course. Heaven forbid. Let's just say that it involves some time alone in bed, thinking in French, and pudding. More to the point, James knows that Christmas calm isn't a great way to start a story, and so she plays against it with delicious conflict.

Any character, whether wholly negative or naïvely positive or somewhere in between, can be alive, alert, and engaged in life. But how is that conveyed to the reader? There are three key techniques: the use of observation, opinions, and self-awareness.

A person who notices things that the rest of us do not is automatically attractive and strong. *I wish I'd seen that!* Ever feel that mild envy when a friend has pointed out something to you? If so, you've felt the effect I'm talking about. Make your characters observant.

Kathryn Stockett's #1 *New York Times* best-seller *The Help* (2009) is about "Skeeter" Phelan, a recent college graduate who shakes up the white world of Jackson, Mississippi, in 1962 by writing a book about their domestic help. Skeeter's the main character, but equal standouts are the maids themselves, most especially peppery Minny Jackson and point-of-view character Aibileen Clark. Indeed, it's Aibileen's voice that opens the novel, in a passage of observation about her employer, Elizabeth Leefolt, who is, let's just say, not a natural mother:

Here's something about Miss Leefolt: she not just frowning all the time, she skinny. Her legs is so spindly, she look like she done growed em last week. Twenty-three years old and she lanky as a fourteen-year-old boy. Even her hair is thin, brown, see-through. She try to tease it up, but it only make it look thinner. Her face be the same shape as that red devil on the redhot candy box, pointy chin and all. Fact, her whole body be so full a sharp knobs and corners, it's no wonder she can't soothe that baby. Babies *like fat*. Like to bury they face up in you armpit and go to sleep. They like big fat legs too. That I know.

Aibileen's not a neutral observer, wouldn't you say? She's got sharp opinions, which sadly she must keep to herself. But her view of the world is entirely her own: raw, unfiltered, full of irony. Editors like to call such a narrative tone "engaging," but I call it honest, strong, and resolute. As I said earlier, strength of character is a foundation of reader care. It's a principle to keep in mind, not only in creating their actions but in building their observations. Make your characters see things we don't; express them in a way we wouldn't. Do that and you'll send your readers on a happy head trip, a wholly legal hallucination.

Opinionated people can be off-putting, but say this for them: They stand for something. They have self-assurance. They're unafraid to put themselves out there, to hell with the consequences. Even when we disagree with them, we respect their ability to deliver their views. We can even enjoy being challenged. Who knows? We might even be persuaded to alter our own thinking.

Earlier in this chapter I mentioned Enzo, the dog narrator of Garth Stein's *The Art of Racing in the Rain*. Enzo is a study in strong point-of-view writing; after all, dogs look at things from a different angle. So it is with Enzo, who has definite opinions on topics from crows to classic movies. He watches a lot of TV while his owner works, you see. He likes the History Channel and ESPN, but his favorite is . . .

> Let me tell you this: The Weather Channel is not about weather;
> it is about the *world!* It is about how weather affects us all, our en-
> tire global economy, health, happiness, spirit. The channel delves
> with great detail into weather phenomena of all different kinds—
> hurricanes, cyclones, tornadoes, monsoons, hail, rain, lightning
> storms—and they especially delight in the confluence of multiple
> phenomena. Absolutely fascinating.

Does it seem to you that Enzo is a mixed breed with a college degree? Or
maybe he's a drop-out, since while he knows words like "confluence," he
doesn't know what to call a nail file. No matter. He's an opinionated pooch,
and that makes this mutt stand out. What about your characters? Do they
have strong opinions? Let them rant once in a while and you won't be slow-
ing your story, you'll be building character. And that's not just my opinion.

If opinions are powerful, one's opinion about oneself may be the most
powerful assertion of all. Self-awareness is really self-assessment: honesty, insight, critical evaluation, generous acceptance. It's not the same, obviously, as self-importance or self-aggrandizement. No one likes a blowhard, but everyone respects a person who can take a hard look at herself
and see the truth.

Abraham Verghese's *Cutting for Stone* (mentioned previously in chapter four) is the story of two brothers, both surgeons, who are separated by
events personal and political in their native Ethiopia. Marion, the novel's
main character, winds up in America where late in the novel he reconnects
with his birth father, a cold British surgeon, who after several months and
some personal revelations suggests they meet at an Ethiopian restaurant
in Manhattan. At the end of this meal, Marion is ready to let go of his anger toward this absent father and see both his father and himself honestly:

> I suppose I understood Thomas Stone's shutting people out. Af-
> ter Genet's betrayal, I never wanted to have such strong feelings
> for a woman again. Not unless I had a written guarantee. I'd en-
> countered a medical student from Mecca, a saint compared with

my first love; she was kind, generous, beautiful, and seemed to transcend herself, as if her existence was secondary to her interest in the world and the things in it, including me. My belated and muted response must have pushed her away, lost me any chance of a future with her. Did I feel sad? Yes. And stupid? Yes, but I also felt relieved. By losing her, I was protecting from her and she from me. I had that in common with this man sitting before me. I thought of a watch that had stopped ticking, and how it showed the correct time twice a day.

Ouch. Self-assessment can hurt, but it's a powerful moment in both life and stories. When in your manuscript does your protagonist see herself clearly? When does he admit the truth to himself? One of the greatest strengths you can give a character is this honesty.

Strongest of all is the courage to monitor oneself: to assess, judge, and render verdicts as events unfold, forthright as a referee during a world championship when everything is on the line. Do you understand yourself a little better every day? Most of us do. So it should be with characters. At first self-measurement might feel extraneous. It doesn't work to advance the story as such, but it does deepen character, which is just as important.

Passionate engagement in life is a powerful tool for making characters gripping, whomever they may be and whatever their disposition, dark or sunny. Use observation, opinions, and self-awareness in building them and you can get away with pretty much anything. Be they extreme, outrageous, or unlike anyone who has ever lived, your readers still will have a way to understand and engage.

WHAT MAKES CHARACTERS UNIVERSAL?

In any literary era, there are trends in characterizations. Whole decades have been defined by characters who were blithe, survivors, or edgy. The evolution of young adult protagonists makes this particularly clear. In the first half of the 20th century, children from Horatio Alger to the Hardy

Boys were plucky and alert with derring-do. In the 1970s, pervasive problem novels celebrated teen angst. More recently, the norm has become snarky detachment. The sociological basis for these changes is fun to debate, but my point is that protagonists are subject to fashion.

For instance, in our time it's highly fashionable for characters to be obsessed. Obsession can imply focus and strength of commitment, but it can also hammer us like a migraine headache. Sometimes it's just a lazy label. When I see the word in query letters I groan, much as I do when protagonists are described as *haunted by demons*. Not again! Perhaps authors are reaching for a shortcut to make queries easier to write, but more likely they've adopted the latest stereotype.

Why do stereotypes fail? The obvious reason is that familiarity has a dulling effect. There's a deeper reason, though. Stereotypical characters aren't authentic. They lack the startling vividness of people who are unlike anyone we've ever known. In fact, I'll go further. Here's a counter-intuitive principle for you to consider: the more unlike anyone else you make a character, the more universal that character will become.

Are you anything like Aibileen Clark, one of the maids in *The Help*? Are you African American? Do you live in Jackson, Mississippi, in 1962? Do you tolerate daily doses of overt racism? Do you ride in the back of the bus to work? Did your son die young? Do you have to scrape by, counting pennies to get by on your forty-three dollars in weekly wages? Do you bite your sharp tongue every day, groveling, dissembling, and lying to keep your job? Do you iron pleats and patiently potty train someone else's child? Have you risked everything you rely on to assist an insecure fledgling author in writing a book that will enrage everyone? Would you bake feces into a pie that you serve to your employer?

I venture to guess that description doesn't fit you. (Am I wrong?) Yet who among us hasn't felt like an outsider, been treated unfairly, scraped by on too little, suffered in a job, yearned for justice, and contemplated revenge? Aibileen is all of us; but oddly, she becomes more iconic the more Stockett makes her different.

There you go. The secret of standout characters is their uniqueness. It can be developed in any number of ways, from their appearance to their opinions. Principles, perplexing quirks, and inner puzzles all can help but too often are shortcuts and substitutes for the harder work of building standout characters from the ground up. Why shirk? You take care with the real people in your own life, true? You puzzle through their odd habits and weird issues to get to the person inside.

Loving your characters is the same commitment but can work in reverse, especially if a character is a lot like you. Understand and empathize first. Then, instead of going easy and relieving the trouble inside, let that trouble twist, warp, and test your character. Push that character to ways of being and behaving that are extreme, unsettling, or just plain out there. There's plenty of time to make things better; hundreds of pages, in fact.

In a way, making a character different than any who's existed before begins with making that character like you, only more so. The store of individuality at your disposal is your own incomparable self. Borrow it, but blow it up. Let yourself loose. The more singular you become on the page, the more your readers will see themselves there, too. Look, we're all crazy, sane, and sublime in the same ways as you. Show that on the page and you make it okay for the rest of us to be our strange and wonderful selves, too.

⊸21ST CENTURY TOOLS⊷

PROTAGONISTS

- Is your protagonist an Everyman or Everywoman? What's his or her outstanding quality? Show it within their first five pages. Terrific. Now show it within one page.

- Is your protagonist a hero or heroine, someone with a job that entails danger, big decisions, and high responsibility? Find one way (even a small one) in which he is perfectly human. Got it? Good. Show it on the page right away.

- Is your protagonist dark, haunted, outcast, suffering, or non-human? In what way does this character most want to become more normal, human, or happy? Show that longing right away.

- Whatever you came up with in the three exercises above, find three new places to reinforce that in the remainder of your manuscript.

LIVING TOGETHER

- What's a foundational attribute of your protagonist? Create an odd tic or habit that implies the opposite. Add six times. *Voilà*: a quirk.

- What can your protagonist do that no one else can? What's one unexpected benefit? What's the biggest cost? When does it not work? Add.

- Give your protagonist a paranormal gift or superpower. If that's un-realistic, scale it to make it possible but eerie, unusual, and hard to explain. Now use it.

- Give your protagonist a handicap. What's the best thing about it? Show that. Get it in the way, or make it inconvenient, three times.

- What's something hard to explain about your protagonist? Deepen the mystery. Make the puzzle more puzzling. Bury the answer deeper. Delay the explanation.
- What does your protagonist know about himself that's true? What does he not see that's even more true? Hit 'em with it.
- Quick: Write down something completely out of character for your protagonist to do. Don't know why she would do that? Better still. Do it. Work out the reason later. (But do work it out.)
- What does your protagonist know about people that no one else does? Create three moments when she spots that in others.
- In your current scene, who's against your protagonist? What's that character hiding? Let your protagonist intuit, guess, or see the truth.
- What does your protagonist love best about the one she loves the most? What's something unflattering about that person that your protagonist sees through? Show and add.
- Pick someone your protagonist knows and interacts with. Where (or who) will that person be in ten years? Give that perspective to your protagonist.
- What does your protagonist believe beyond all else? Create a story event that forces him to accept the opposite.
- Find a small hurt someone suffers. What's the big principle or hidden injustice it represents? Stir your protagonist to anger over it.
- What happens in your story that makes your protagonist the most angry? Anticipate that anger three times in the story before the big event.
- During a big dramatic event, what's one small thing your point-of-view character realizes will never change—or never be the same again?
- Find a small passing moment in your manuscript. What big meaning does your protagonist see in it? Add that.
- Find a moment for your protagonist to rise above it all. Let her rise. Show it.

- What's the most selfless thing your protagonist does? What positive effect does it have, or what change does it provoke, in someone unexpected? Add that.
- Why does your protagonist's life matter? At the moment when that's most true, allow your protagonist to humbly grasp his importance to someone else or to the great scheme of things.
- What is your antagonist's most selfless motive? What motivates him for the good? Add that.
- Create a selfless action for your antagonist. Add it.

THE GOOD IN THE BAD

- What's the worst thing your antagonist must do? Make it against her principles. Make it unthinkable. Then make it imperative.
- What's your antagonist's goal, objective, yearning, hope, or dream? What six practical steps are needed to achieve that? What are the biggest blocks? Add all.
- Find three new times and ways to bring your protagonist and antagonist face to face. (If your protagonist doesn't meet this character until late in the game, then that's not your day-to-day, working antagonist.)
- What does your antagonist believe in? Who else shares those values? Why is your antagonist actually right? When does your protagonist see that, too?
- What does your antagonist most want to bring about? How is that something that everyone wants? Explain and add.
- What do you like best about your antagonist? Demonstrate that in the biggest way possible.
- What is your antagonist missing? What hasn't she seen, figured out, or yet found? Give that insight. Grant that discovery.
- In what way (big or small) is your antagonist like you? Show that one time.

SECONDARY CHARACTERS

- Pick a secondary character allied to your protagonist. What's the biggest way in which she is different? Show it.
- Same character: When does she most understand and best love your protagonist? Show it. When does she least understand and hate your protagonist? Demonstrate it.
- Same character: What contradiction does this character embody? What's the biggest way in which we can see that?
- Same character: What's the most important piece of shared history this character has with your protagonist? What can your protagonist count on? What's the article of trust between them? Shatter it. Then repair it.
- Same character: What does this character see about your protagonist that your protagonist denies? Force a showdown over it.
- Same character: How can this character betray your protagonist? Do it.
- Same character: What self-sacrifice can this character make for your protagonist? Make it.
- Before a new character arrives on stage, give your protagonist an expectation or fear with regard to that character. Make the reality three times better or worse.

WARM AND ALIVE

- Find a spot where your protagonist is in a black mood. Objectify it. How is this blackness different than any other? What does it look like? Why does it feel good to feel bad? Will it blow over? When? Create a passage in which your protagonist studies her own misery.
- Find your character in a sunny state. Qualify this bliss. Why can't this ebullience be trusted? What's the cloud on the horizon? What shouldn't be forgotten? Create a passage in which you cast doubt upon good times.

- Where's your protagonist right now? Look around. Let him notice something that no one else does: something about the place, the people, or the atmosphere itself. Get it down.
- Give your protagonist passionate feelings about something trivial: e.g., cappuccino, bowling, argyle socks. Write his rant. Add it.
- In your current scene, what's a setting detail that delights or disgusts your POV character? Why? Add it.
- In your current scene, what does your protagonist feel about someone or something else that's rude, inconvenient, or just out there? Go on, protagonist: Blurt it out. Whoops.
- In your current scene, what's the hidden high principle that your protagonist sees at work? Express it. Make the action show it more.
- In the last inner monologue you wrote, insert one insight, question, or worry that hasn't hit you (or your protagonist) before now.
- You are your protagonist's best friend. Big or small, what's safe for your protagonist to share with you right now? Add it immediately.
- From your protagonist's point of view, list: 1) the best thing about the problem at hand 2) the secret enemy 3) the best place to think things over 4) the problem with authority 5) who needs help more than anyone else. Add those things.
- Pick a spot in the middle; ask your protagonist: 1) What score would you award yourself right now? 2) What are your chances of success? 3) What don't you have that's needed to win? Add it.
- What's the biggest thing your protagonist needs to know about herself? Give her three good reasons not to care . . . then tear those down.
- If your protagonist is content with himself, give him fifteen minutes of self-assessment. How would others see him? What needs improvement?
- If your protagonist is unhappy with himself, give him one good thing to appreciate. Find the moment for "maybe I'm not so bad after all."

- What's the worst thing that happens to your protagonist? Work backwards. Make it something he has spent a lifetime avoiding.
- What's the emotion or experience you're most afraid to put your protagnist through? Go there. Do it. Now.

WHAT MAKES CHARACTERS UNIVERSAL?

- List the ways in which your protagonist is like anyone. Go down the list. How many specific ways can you make your protagonist different?
- Write your protagonist's biography. Go over it. Make his childhood in some way weird. What's one odd habit she had in adolescence? What's a peculiar aspect of adulthood?
- Give your protagonist a signature fashion look, an uncanny gift for a certain game, a knack for an offbeat sport, vast knowledge of something special . . . anything remarkable.
- What's something about your protagonist that most people wouldn't know? What's one outward clue to it that—until you understand—is decidedly odd? Add it.
- What's your protagonist's big unresolved issue? Find a new way for it to twist your protagonist.
- What situation would test your protagonist the most? How would it hit her biggest weakness? What are you waiting for?
- In what way are you a little crazy? What do you see more clearly than others? What was your best moment? Can you give any of that to your protagonist? You can? Do it.

06:
THE THREE LEVELS OF STORY

THE BREAKDOWN

Most novelists understand, at least theoretically, the need for a main problem or central conflict. It's the iron skeleton that holds up the skyscraper. If it's in there, the thing will not collapse, right?

Similarly, most novelists understand that an individual scene needs a goal, turning point, change, or just something to happen to justify that scene's existence. A strong scene will, like an anchor, keep a reader from drifting away through many chapters ahead, right?

Less well understood is the necessity of constant line-by-line tension to compel readers to turn pages. Those who get the idea, though, often believe that what generates disquiet in readers is limited to physical action or pure danger. In *The Fire in Fiction* (2009), I argued that the foundations of micro-tension are more complex. More and more fiction writers get that they need micro-tension in their novels, I'm happy to say, but sadly many continue to imagine that it's like adding jalapeño peppers to an omelet: a little goes a long way.

Wrong on all counts.

The truth is that only when all three levels of story are working *all the time* do novels genuinely keep readers under their spells. A deeply absorbing story isn't magic. It's a beat kept steady by a masterful drummer whose hands and feet are operating independently yet also together. Like an infectious rock rhythm, its drive is multi-layered and constant, even when it seems to pause.

THE PROBLEM WITH PLOT

Plot-driven novelists might seem to have it easy. Their stories impose structure. If there's a murder, someone's got to investigate. Saving the world also means action: Locate the villain, get there in time, overcome obstacles. Fantasy involves a journey; urban fantasy is a battle. Even less rigid formats like romance, horror, and so on have requirements and conventions to help.

Writers of literary fiction, women's fiction, and other character-driven stories might appear to have a tougher assignment. Working up the substance of their stories can feel a bit like hammering together cotton candy to make the framework of a house.

There are many templates one can use in organizing and planning a novel. The simplest is to define a main problem, complicate it, orchestrate to a climax, and resolve everything at the end. If that's too plain, one can conceptualize a novel as onion layers, frame-and-flashback, hide-and-seek, healing-and-self-discovery, past-and-present, Cinderella, Hero's Journey, whodunit, three-act structure, tragedy, comedy, satire, disaster, or any number of other patterns. You can think of action as rising, falling, running in parallel, or coming full circle. If you are geometry-minded, you can even describe plots as spheres, cubes, or cones.

In his marvelous book *20 Master Plots (And How to Build Them)* (1993), Ronald B. Tobias extrapolated some useful plot patterns including adventure, escape, revenge, The Riddle, transformation, forbidden love, and wretched excess. Wow! If you need more specific directions, there are paint-by-number, fill-in-the-blank software programs and workbooks like Evan Marshall's *The Marshall Plan for Novel Writing* (2001). Useful for beginners, most pros eschew such crutches.

Or do they? As I mentioned, genre writers often lean on the conventions of various sub-genres to help generate the substance of their stories. In the fantasy field alone there are distinct requirements for quest, urban, assassin, humorous, historical, multi-cultural, anthropomorphic, and dark fantasy. The romance field has a vast number of sub-genres; so do the fields of mystery, thriller, science fiction, and young adult. Take your pick. Or don't bother yourself with grubby formulae. Hack your way through to your own unique story type. Hey, it only took God six days. (He rested on the seventh.)

If you are a literary, organic, character-driven sort of novelist, then you probably strive to be original, or at most *to work in the tradition of* someone else. You'll let critics guess at your *influences*.

Fine.

The truth is that both plot- and character-driven novelists often have identical issues: 1) the engine of their stories, the premise, is low-horsepower; 2) the middle of the story doesn't have enough happening. What's supposed to be constantly escalating drama turns out to be an ever-rising landfill. Addressing one issue does not take care of the other. Both need separate attention.

THE POWER IN PREMISE

There is today a fashion for fiction that's *high concept*. It's easy to see why it appeals: its grip is quick, it's easy to pitch, and it provides the author a degree of security. *A high-concept story is sure-fire, no fail, a lock!* That result, of course, is not automatic. The promise of a high-concept premise can quickly dissolve. A manuscript is like a racecar poised at the edge of the Bonneville Salt Flats. It takes more than a high-octane blast off to propel that baby all the way across the desert.

High concept is also no help to novelists for whom writing is an exploration, a process of drafting and redrafting. What are organic writers supposed to do when their starting point is no more than a scrap, an image, or an intention? Can't a premise be something that's grown and identified later, like a virus in a Petri dish?

A strong premise can emerge organically after many drafts, of course, but the challenge there is to write something that will coalesce. Finding focus can be tricky. The trick, though, is to use tests and measures to help discard what's weak and retain what's strong.

In *Writing the Breakout Novel* (2002), I argued that powerful premise is plausible (or becomes plausible), has inherent conflict, is original, and has gut emotional appeal. Those qualities can be missing in a high concept, especially the first and last ones. Those same values also are useful tests and measures to apply to the raw material in organically grown drafts.

You can give any premise the durability and forward thrust of a jet engine by working on its inherent conflict. When the conflict built into the very foundation of a novel is strong, maybe even irresolvable, it will take a heck of a lot of story to work it out.

Erin Morgenstern's debut *The Night Circus* (2011) is a literary fantasy that won the kind of critical attention that hard genre fantasists envy (or tellingly disdain). Her central creation, the mysterious and nocturnal *Le Cirque des Rêves*, is irresistible candy for its addicted followers. The story's main characters are two children, Marco and Celia, illusionists who are raised to be competitors unto death, the better to enhance the circus's dark allure. That's fine enough for plot purposes, but Morgenstern then builds in an irreconcilable conflict: Marco and Celia fall in love. Their hearts are thus at odds with their destinies, an inherent conflict that demands considerable groundwork be laid for credibility, and which will take quite a bit of story to resolve.

Originality doesn't mean inventing a story format that's brand new. That's impossible. It does mean devising devious twists to familiar formulae. Reversing expectations is the best way, but giving any element of a story an unconventional aspect will help.

Why are teens preoccupied with death? In case you haven't noticed, young adult literature is littered with dead kids. *Do-over novels* like Lauren Oliver's *Before I Fall* (2010) and Gayle Forman's *If I Stay* (2009) put their protagonists through *Groundhog-Day*-like reruns to measure their lives and make sense of their deaths. Jay Asher's *New York Times* best-seller and highly lauded *Thirteen Reasons Why* (2007) also takes an unconventional approach to this familiar topic. Teen girl Hannah Baker has committed suicide. Two weeks later her friend Clay Jensen receives a package of cassette tapes recorded by Hannah before her death, explaining the thirteen reasons why she killed herself. Knowing he will figure in her story, Clay listens as Hannah narrates the tale of how she got a reputation she didn't deserve. Her catalogue of petty high school meanness isn't wholly awful: some friends like Clay cared . . . they just didn't care enough.

So affecting is Asher's novel that it's easy to miss its neat reversal of a familiar formula. In mystery novels, there's a death. Someone figures out whodunit. In Asher's novel there's a death, but it's the dead person who reveals the truth. There's no sleuth: Hannah Baker is her own detective. This might have been just a shallow gimmick, but Asher uses his backwards-mystery structure to tease high suspense from a known conclusion.

If your raw material is a mess, you can ask yourself which parts of the story *get* to you. The stuff that stirs you up emotionally is the important stuff. The strongest responses for which we're wired are the ones with gut emotional appeal. An act of betrayal, forgiveness, surrender to love, the death of a child . . . we could go on. The point is to find that gut-grabbing material and find a way for it to become primary to your story. Make it either the inciting or climactic event. Work until everything else that happens in some way radiates from that, or, alternately, drags your characters inexorably into its gravity well.

Gut-grabbing story ideas can arise from family history, obscure news stories, or intriguing footnotes discovered during research, but in fact that serendipity isn't needed. Sometimes all you need is a simple human fear or desire, something that any of us might feel. For instance, do you worry what would happen to you if your spouse suddenly died or was taken from you? Have you ever fantasized about being a hero; say, if you had a chance to save someone from being killed? The American master of gutgrabbing stories is Dean Koontz, who used those very premises in *The Husband* (2006) and *The Good Guy* (2007). What if you could know your future? Koontz also built a gripping story out of this common fantasy in *Life Expectancy* (2004).

In *Life Expectancy*, a self-described "lummox" named Jimmy Tock is cursed with foreknowledge not of his whole life but of five specific days that will be "terrible." This forecast is made by his dying grandfather on the night Jimmy is born. The grandfather's raving is given instant credibility because he not only predicts Jimmy's exact minute of birth and weight, but also reveals that Jimmy will have syndactyly (fused digits) and because he warns, "Don't trust the clown." Sure enough, in the expectant fathers' waiting room is a demented circus clown whose wife is giving birth. The clown goes on a shooting spree, and thus Jimmy Tock lives his life knowing that the five terrible days are inescapable. And, boy, are they terrible. Koontz, a maniacal plotter, makes sure that his arresting premise pays off throughout his novel's middle.

Plausible stories have a *that-could-happen-to-me* quality. Now, this might come as news to authors of fantasy, horror, thrillers, dystopian YA, adventure, and other essentially impossible stories. How do such authors keep us enthralled when their stories are essentially ridiculous? They do it by making the humans in it feel real. When that is effectively done, we imagine ourselves slaying monsters, saving the world, staying alive against high odds, and other unlikely outcomes.

A reality-based story has the opposite challenge. Its characters and their worlds are already easy to imagine. You would think that would make readers automatically identify. Not necessarily true. No one is deeply engaged by same old, same old. For a reality-based story to stir readers' imaginations it needs to test characters in the extreme, pushing them over the edge into actions we normally would rule out. In other words, a reality-based story is best when its story events are, to some extent, unreal.

Chris Cleave's *Little Bee* (2008) is not a genre novel. It's not built around a murder, romance, or the supernatural. It's a real-world story, except that what happens in the world of its heroine, London fashion magazine editor Sarah O'Rourke, is unreal. Sarah's life is tied to that of a Nigerian refugee whose host and protector she improbably becomes. Indeed, she literally chops off the middle finger of her left hand to try to save Little Bee.

Wait, a fashion magazine editor chops off her middle finger for an African girl? On the face of it, this central and inciting incident is pretty far-fetched. Cleave, however, knows this. He realizes that for his readers to swallow this unlikely occurrence he has to lay a lot of groundwork. It has to be believable that a London fashion editor and her husband would holiday on a Nigerian delta where conflict over oil has boiled into near anarchic violence. It has to be credible that a Nigerian girl could make her way to England and find them in suburban Kingston-upon-Thames. There has to be a true bond between two women who could not be more different. It's a tall order.

Cleave tackles these challenges with high storytelling skill. Sarah O'Rourke is carefully built as the kind of iconoclastic woman who founds a fashion magazine with the idea of using sexy allure to trick readers into reading articles of real substance. She's a woman who marries an Irish columnist for the *Times* because he's not her usual type. She's just the kind of woman who, to be different and weirdly hip, would decide to take a marriage-reviving holiday at a Nigerian beach resort because, well, why not?

It's that fateful whim that leads to Sarah and her husband taking a beach walk beyond the boundaries of safety just as two Nigerian girls, fleeing their village after a slaughter, are tracked to the beach by mercenaries who intend to kill them because they were witnesses. The dramatic events on the beach, and Sarah's hopeless, naïve, and doomed *Sophie's Choice* decision to chop off a finger, are not as big a stretch as Little Bee's later arrival on her doorstep. But this, too, Cleave works to make believable. He does this by spending a large chunk of the novel's first half portraying Little Bee's release from two years in a UK detention center. Released with Little Bee are several other women whose stories serve to sensitize the reader to the plight of refugees. Their stories are so extreme, their need so great, and their chances so slender that it makes perfect sense that Little Bee would use Sarah's husband's business card as a lifeline, turning up on Sarah's doorstep just days after her husband has killed himself.

Plausibility, in other words, is something earned. For a novel to draw readers into an unreal world, or to make unreal events something readers could see happening to themselves, is a challenge to be met. But that's the job. Tackle that job in earnest and whatever type of story you're telling, the reward is a reading experience that readers will not only buy into, but which they'll live for themselves.

MANAGING THE MIDDLE

After you've strengthened the foundation of your story, you face the hard work of building the middle. Most sag. Not enough happens. The central conflict is not pushed terribly far. The main problem doesn't become extreme. For virtually all novelists, the challenge is to push farther, go deeper, and get mean and nasty.

For plot-driven storytellers, filling out the middle is essentially a process of making the main problem worse, and worse, and finally impossible to solve. Whatever your protagonist is trying to do (or avoid), ask how many things can possibly go wrong, then make every one of those disasters occur. Call those events, setbacks, complications, obstacles, or whatever you like. Regardless of your terminology, recognize that you need more of them.

Character-driven stories have the same challenge, but in that case the problem to be compounded is internal. The process essentially is to define the new state of being toward which your protagonist is moving, then set him back in every way imaginable. Most writers don't. To overcome your own resistance, ask what if your character is utterly unable get what she needs, seeks, desires, or yearns for? What if she nevertheless absolutely must have it? What's every last thing she can try? Make a list. Include the biggest, craziest, most extreme, utterly desperate thing she can do when pushed to the limit.

Go there. Go beyond. Make it fail. Then push even further toward the inner desire. Does it feel like you're getting melodramatic? The problem with most character-driven manuscripts is not that they go over the top but that they aim too low. They underwhelm. Events are not dramatic enough. Surprise and delight are in shortly supply because the author is too polite, restrained, style-conscious, or afraid to incite a riot.

Téa Obreht's *The Tiger's Wife* (2011) was a winner of the Orange Prize for Fiction and has gone on to best-seller status around the world. It's the story of Natalia, the granddaughter of a man in a Balkan state. A doctor, she is visiting orphanages after a recent war when she learns of the death of her grandfather, who may have died searching for the "deathless man," an immortal vagabond of folklore. Seeking the truth of this, Natalia recalls the stories her grandfather told her, especially the story of a zoo tiger that escaped during a German bombardment in 1941, terrorized her grandfather's village one winter, and befriended a mysterious deaf-mute woman. The hunt for the fearsome tiger is portrayed with high drama. See what you think:

> After uttering a little prayer, the blacksmith did actually raise the gun to his shoulder, and did cock it, sight, and pull the trigger, and the gun did go off, with a blast that rocked the clearing and spasmed through the blacksmith's knees. But when the smoke cleared and the noise of it had died down in his ribs, the blacksmith looked up to discover that the tiger was on its feet and moving swiftly to the frozen center of the pond, undeterred by the ice and the men and the sound of the gunshot. Out of the corner of his eye, he saw Luka drop his pitchfork and break for cover. The blacksmith fell to his knees. His hand was rummaging through the clots of fear and the buttons and crumbs that lined the bottom of his pocket, searching for the encased bullet. When he found it, he stuffed it into the muzzle with shaking hands that seemed to be darting everywhere with the sheer force of terror, and fumbled for the ramrod. The tiger was almost over the pond, bounding on muscles like springs. He heard Jovo muttering, "Fuck me," helplessly, and the sound of Jovo's footsteps moving away. The blacksmith had the ramrod out and he was shoving it into the muzzle, pumping and pumping and pumping furiously, his hand already on the trigger, and he was ready to fire, strangely calm with the tiger there, almost on him, its whiskers so close and surprisingly bright and rigid. At last, it was done, and he tossed the ramrod aside and peered into the barrel, just to be sure, and blew off his own head with a thunderclap.

Quiet literary writing? I'd say not! But remember this won the Orange Prize and was a National Book Award finalist. Subtle and understated aren't always the way to go. Sometimes big emotions ("terror") and dramatic events ("blew off his own head") are stronger. The power of dreams lies in their surreal distortion of life. So it is with stories. Mirroring life is fine, but blowing it up to the proportion of myth is the way to make high impact.

In life we act nicely, but our secret desire is to scream, insult, rebel, destroy, declare, confess, seduce, indulge, lavish, wake up, stay up, get drunk, go berserk, see truth, tear down, shame everyone, lift ourselves, and generally mess things up in a fine old catharsis. Don't you ever want to yell, *"Fuck you!"* to everyone you've ever known? Or say to them, *"Damn, you people are beautiful!"*? Did it take alcohol to get you to that point? Why not instead get drunk on the possibilities for your story?

This is your chance. This is what fiction is for. Or rather, that's what your characters are for. They are your proxies and our mirror. Make the mirror one from a fun house. Distort, fracture, bend, and bloat. It's still an honest image, just one that's more interesting, absorbing, thought provoking, and complex than that flat 6 A.M. honesty we get from our bathroom mirror every morning.

STRONG SCENES

I often hear authors talking about scene and sequel, high and low points, rise and fall. The screenwriting term *beats* sometimes creeps into story discussions, too. There are many terms available to help conceptualize the unfolding of a story, but are they useful?

Sure, as useful as any metaphor can be, but such analogies can lead authors into the false assurance that the lulls between high moments, the caesuras after a "beat," aftermath scenes, and empty travel sequences are not only okay, but necessary elements of novel structure.

They're not.

The bricks of story are scenes. Every scene builds the story one incremental step. How? There are a lot of ways to look at them. The most common starting point is to pick the point-of-view character, then to determine that character's immediate goal. The character then achieves that goal, tastes disaster, receives new information, and/or gets booted off in a new direction.

No doubt that vanilla structure feels too plain. Where's the atmosphere, hidden currents, sly buildup, misdirection, action, revelation, back-and-forth, turnabout, low point, and all the other cool stuff that makes scenes artful? Create your own shopping list. One of the most efficient indexes of elements I've run across is found in mystery author Nancy Pickard's book (written with Lynn Lott), *Seven Steps on the Writer's Path* (2004). Her essential scene elements have an acronym, *CASTS*: conflict, action, surprise, turn, and senses. Not bad. Borrow it if it helps.

As one who starves at a feast of better than a thousand raw manuscript scenes every year, I can tell you that most scenes offer little nourishment. It's not just that they're too long and not tense enough. It's that they don't deliver a profound feeling of change.

Plot-driven authors feel they're doing that if they drop a surprise or cook up a cliffhanger, a supposed bombshell of a plot turn that's meant to blow my mind but at most lifts one eyebrow. Character-driven authors try to do the same thing with feelings, seeking to demolish me with a scene's devastating emotional force, but by and large leaving me maybe mildly moved or even ice cold.

Power and drama accrue in scenes that change both the story circumstances and the focal character, too. They work inwardly and outwardly. Action has extra meaning when it springs from and reveals a character's inner state. The inner state is just a dull, static landscape painting until it's brought to life and given outward movement.

Now look—if you're a literary novelist, don't panic. Big things don't need to happen in every scene. Inner shifts can be small. But don't fool yourself: If there isn't a noticeable outward externalization of the inner shift, your scene will be weak. Plot-driven writers have the reverse worry: bogging down their scenes with too much gooey interiority. That's understandable, but action by itself is hollow. Only when its inner meaning comes clear to the participant do you get high impact.

These conjoined effects are most clearly present in a great scene's inner and outer turning points. The *outer turning point* is the precise second when the focal character's circumstances actually change. The *inner turning point* is the way in which what's happened is changing the point of view character's self-understanding.

Crime writer Laura Lippman has cool control of her scenes. Following seven mysteries featuring Baltimore detective Tess Monaghan, Lippman began alternating series titles and stand-alones in 2003. *What the Dead Know* (2007) hinges on the thirty-year-old disappearance of two sisters from a shopping mall. In the present, a raving hit-and-run driver claims to be one of the missing sisters; but she's unstable and lying, at least in part. Unscrambling this cold case falls to police detective Kevin Infante, who is your typical detective: hard-shelled; personal life a mess. In his introductory scene he wakes up in the bed of a woman whose name he struggles (successfully) to remember, but it gets worse:

> His eyes flicked around the room, searching for a clock but also taking in his surroundings. A bedroom, of course, and a reasonably nice one, with arty posters of flowers and what his ex-wife, the more recent one, always called a color scheme, which was supposed to be a good thing, but it never sounded right to Infante. A scheme was a plot, a plan to get away with something. But then a color scheme was part of a trap, too, if you thought about it, the one that began with a too-expensive ring, revolving credit at Shofer's, and a mortage payment, then ended—twice in his experience so far—in a Baltimore County courtroom, with the woman taking all the stuff and leaving all the debt. The scheme here was pale yellow and green, not in the least objectionable, but it made him feel vaguely nauseous. As he sorted his clothes from hers, he began noticing other odd details about the room, things that didn't quite track. The built-in desk beneath the casement window, the boxy minifridge draped with a cloth, a small

microwave on top of that, the pennant above the desk, extolling the Towson Wildcats . . . *Fuck me*, he thought. *Fuck me.*

"So," he said. "What's your major?"

Oops. A college girl, waaay too young. It would be easy to let the scene go at that: jerk of a detective, stupidly stuck in a downward spiral. But Lippman is too skilled to keep the moment flat. Infante's deduction of her age is the scene's turning point. Infante is shamed. The girl, dubbed a "Debbie," scowls. Infante departs and is that morning assigned to reopen the cold case of the Bethany sisters. As he contemplates it, though, he cannot help wondering, *What the fuck did I do to piss off Debbie?*

Now, that smidgen of self-examination isn't much, I'll admit. But it's the scene's inner turning point. Infante isn't as big a jerk as we imagine. He is now shown to care, at least a little, which is good because the twisty case of the Bethany sisters will cause him to care a lot. The turning point here is all the more effective for being under-played. (Literary types take note.)

Pinning down the inner and outer turning points in any given scene is the easiest way to make sure that the scene is having a strong effect. When every scene is enacting change, inside and out, you won't have to worry about lulls, pauses, or aftermath. It won't matter what type of scene you're working on. Even if you've opted (against my advice) for a scene that is introductory, marking time, or making tea, every scene will advance your story.

SCENE ENHANCEMENTS

Needless to say, it takes more than that to make a scene great. Scenes need setting, atmosphere, and mood. They are most memorable when they work surprises, turnabouts, and reversals. Most scenes also are too slow; they need a snappier pace, an efficiency that can be achieved with more effective use of dialogue.

Settings spring alive when they're built of less obvious details. But who sees that which isn't obvious? It has to be your point-of-view character. It's the same thing with atmosphere and mood. In the 21ˢᵗ century, these (for the most part) aren't objective qualities. They're the perceptions of someone on the page.

I said earlier that cliffhangers are only momentarily attention-grabbing gimmicks. That doesn't mean they aren't useful. Surprises, turnabouts, and reversals, like plot twists and turns, are based on a violation of readers' expectations. In other words, what matters is how expectations are set up in the first place.

David Liss is known for the financial flavor of his 18th century historical thrillers. The opening of *The Devil's Company* (2009) finds his proto-detective, Benjamin Weaver, hired to execute a con in a fashionable gaming club called Kingsley's Coffeehouse. With the help of a card dealer, he is supposed to engage a certain card sharp named Robert Bailor in a cacho game of escalating stakes. When Bailor is on the hook for a ruinous sum, the cards will turn against him. In the novel's long opening chapter, Liss details the elaborate execution of the sting. Weaver dresses to offend, insults Bailor, provokes a duel of cards, drinks too much, all the while playing an over-confident rube. Bailor takes the bait. Weaver plays his part with glee, since after all he is gambling (and losing) someone else's money.

When the time comes for the sting to go down, though, the cards do not run the right way. Weaver is unaccountably cleaned out. He must now report to his client, a mystery man named Jerome Cobb, that he has lost eleven hundred pounds of his money. Worse, on his way out he is stopped by Bailor, who has a message:

> He said nothing for a moment, but only gazed upon me. Then he leaned forward as if to salute my cheek, but instead he whispered some words in my ear. "I believe, Mr. Weaver," he said, addressing me by my true name, "that you have now felt the long reach of Jerome Cobb."

A twist on the very message that Weaver was supposed to deliver to Bailor! The truth hits home: The object of the sting was, after all, not Bailor but our hero. The con man has been conned. And so have we. The surprise at the end of this opening chapter is all the more effective because our expectations have been led skillfully in the opposite direction.

By the way, why has Weaver been conned? With a phantom debt now pinned to him, Weaver is blackmailed by Jerome Cobb. In the start of a twisty game of intrigue, Weaver is commanded to steal documents from the all-powerful British East India Company. But is Cobb good or bad? The complex truth unfolds in a tale of conspiracy, corporate warfare, spying, and outcomes difficult to guess.

Dialogue is the highly-geared motor that can speed scenes along, but sadly many novelists are afraid to put their feet on the gas pedal.

I've often wondered why that is. I suspect the hang-up derives from the urgent need to accumulate pages. Many novelists set themselves daily goals, pressuring themselves to hit a certain quota of words. Thus, when at the keyboard it's not quite clear what should come next, authors nevertheless keep typing, filling up pages in order to feel like they're making progress. Tightening is saved for a revision draft, but by then the words have set like cement. They're chipped away but only reluctantly, because every word subtracted means work wasted and a shorter manuscript.

The truth is that a tight and snappy dialogue exchange can often do the work of several pages of prose. But it's fearful to let dialogue predominate. If you do, how are you going to fill up the rest of the scene? Think of it, though, as making space for more to happen.

Loren D. Estleman is one of our most prolific and under-appreciated novelists. In *Gas City* (2007), he departs from his habitual beat, Detroit, to create a Midwestern city infected with corruption. For thirty years the police chief, Francis X. Russell, has been taking bribes from the local crime lord to stay out of a vice district known as The Circle. When Russell's wife

Marty dies, he has a change of heart and determines to clean up Gas City, which naturally proves difficult and dangerous.

For the story to make sense, Chief Russell's motivation needs to be strong; in particular, we need to see the strength of Russell's relationship with his wife if we are to understand how her death could change him. This is hinted at early on in a hospital conversation between Russell and his priest, Hugh Dungannon, immediately after Russell's wife dies. Dungannon asks him about the funeral service:

> Russell shook his head. He was only half listening. "Marty had a poem she liked. By Rossetti."
>
> "I'll use it. Christina?"
>
> "Dante Gabriel. From *The House of Life*. 'As when two men have loved a woman well,' is how it starts."
>
> The leonine face smoothed out. "I didn't think she'd remember."
>
> "She never mentioned it. Not once in thirty-seven years."
>
> "You married a saint."
>
> "She was a blowtop. She threw a skillet at me once."
>
> "I'd have thought she'd be more original."
>
> "It seemed inspired enough at the time. I earned it, I guess. I never was much in the husband department."
>
> "She knew when you married she'd have to share you with the city."
>
> "The city didn't get any bargain, either."
>
> "She died, Francis. You didn't kill her."

Look at how much Estleman accomplishes in that short, economical dialogue exchange. In Russell's complaint we see the opposite: How much Marty meant to him. From Dungannon's insight and compassion we get the long and rich friendship these two men have built. Did you also pick up the long-ago relationship that Russell's wife must have had with Dungannon? Estleman might have elaborated all of that in a long back story chapter. That's what a less secure writer would do. But Estleman is a pro. He knows that twelve lines of dialogue can tell a whole tale.

Sometimes you don't need a scene at all. It's just as well to summarize your way through a span of time. How do you know when to do that? Do it when during that span in a character's experience nothing changes.

Most scenes have a clear start and finish, usually demarked by a space or chapter break. When instead of hard breaks, scenes flow with transitional material to link them, that's a sequence. Are sequences a good idea? Sometimes, but in my experience it's easy to overuse them. For the most part it's stronger to build a story of individual bricks rather than flowing sand. There's a clearer sense of progress.

If you are an organic, exploring kind of author, you may be wondering how you can know if any given section you're working on is advancing the story. *Is this scene doing anything?* To a degree, if you are asking the question, then the answer probably is no.

To pin a scene down, focus on what physically happens. What we feel is amplified by what we can visualize and hear. Push toward change. Follow your fear. (More on this in chapter eight.) Your fear is a compass pointing you toward what's concrete, active, outward, and irrevocable.

MICRO-TENSION

It happens at every workshop. After the presenter explains the methods of constant line-by-line tension and demonstrates how it's done by sparking up several randomly chosen manuscript pages, hands shoot up. An anxious participant asks, "Can there be *too* much tension in a manuscript?"

No.

Let me be clear about that.

No.

When you think you have overloaded a manuscript with tension, you probably have created just enough to hang on to your reader. What feels like too much to you is barely enough. If you don't believe me, try this: With a pencil in hand, open any average novel and begin to read. Put a tick in the margin when your eyes begin to skim down the page. Draw a margin arrow at the spot where you reenter the story flow. How much are you skimming?

The parts that you skim have low tension. When readers encounter that in your own work, they do exactly what you do: skim. Horrifying, isn't it? Especially if that reader is the agent you're hoping to land or the editor who may give you a contract.

You want your readers to read every word, of course, but to do that you need to make magnets of your pages. You need to run an electric current through them. That electricity is micro-tension.

Here's how it works. When you create in your reader an unconscious apprehension, anxiety, worry, question, or uncertainty, then the reader will unconsciously seek to relieve that uneasiness. And there's only one way to do that: Read the next thing on the page.

A constant stream of tension causes readers to read every word of a novel. When they do, we illogically call that novel a *page turner*. The term suggests rapid reading, if not skimming, but it's really the opposite. It means reading with close attention.

AT. TENSION.

It's tempting to limit tension to danger or plot turns. It's even easier to dismiss the whole idea of micro-tension, especially if your purpose is literary. If it is, "tension" probably sounds to you like "explosion." But remember that tension has many degrees of temperature. There's simmering, under-the-surface tension as well as high explosive force. It's even possible to generate apprehension in readers through a deft and devious choice of words; that is, through a disquiet in your language alone.

When a novelist is able to keep you reading even while there's nothing apparently "happening" in a scene, count on it: there's micro-tension at work. Conversely, when you're reading a high-action sequence and, against all logic, it's unexciting, then micro-tension is absent.

Action doesn't generate tension? Not by itself. This misapprehension was brought home to me one day when I taught a workshop for Chi Libris, an organization of published authors of Christian fiction. A participant offered a paragraph from a work-in-progress in which a cougar carried a toddler across a stream (in its mouth, in case you were wondering), pursued by the story's protagonist.

The passage was well written, visually clear—and not particularly scary. When I asked, "What do you think will happen next?" hardly anyone cared. I then asked, "How can we add tension?" Initially, the suggestions focused on making the cougar more menacing, raising the stakes (*the toddler is a senator's child!*), changing the protagonist's actions, etc. Still no one cared.

Then came a suggestion that held the key to increasing tension: Heighten the emotions of the point-of-view character. Even better, create conflicting emotions. Bingo. Suddenly the moment sprang to life. Both the interest level and uncertainty of the outcome spiraled up.

Well, except for a group of male authors clustered in a back row. "But what if the cougar reared up on its hind legs?" "Cougars have vicious fangs; what if its lips curled back?" The guys didn't want to let go of the idea that tension comes from claws.

Finally, I improvised a version of the passage that went something like this:

The cougar splashed across the stream, the toddler limp in its jaws. Jim splashed after it, snapping off a branch. No way was he backing down. Forget it. It was man against nature. And this time man was going to win.

Simple as that was, interest increased. Someone noticed that the hero's determination was undercut by the words *this time*. Another participant wondered, "What happened *last* time?" Exactly. It's the contrast between Jim's bravado and his fear (both implied, please notice) that makes the outcome uncertain, thus forcing the reader to go to the next paragraph on the page.

Light bulbs went off all over the room . . . except, I'm sorry to report, in the back row. "But seriously, what if the cougar . . ." I shook my head in despair. "It's not the cougar, guys," I said. "It's the emotions."

Chapter eight of my book *The Fire in Fiction* is a long, detailed discussion of the operation of micro-tension in a variety of story situations in which it's quite often lacking: dialogue, action, exposition, weather, and landscape openings, back-story, aftermath, travel, violence, sex, description, passages of pure emotion, foreshadowing, and moments in which nothing at all is going on. The unifying principle of micro-tension in almost all those situations is conflicting emotions. Illogical as it sounds, tension arises not from what's outside but from what's inside.

Robert Goolrick's #1 *New York Times* best-selling novel *A Reliable Wife* (2009) concerns a well-to-do businessman, Ralph Truitt, the richest man in his Wisconsin town in 1907. Also the loneliest. Following the death of his Italian wife, he has for twenty years been reclusive and withdrawn. Now, though, he has decided to rejoin the world. He has advertised in newspapers for a "reliable wife," and as the novel opens he is standing on the train station platform waiting with other citizens of the town for the train bringing the "simple honest woman," once a missionary, with whom he has corresponded and whom he hopes will be right for him.

The train is late. Truitt waits, painfully aware of the townspeople watching him. This inactive, waiting, standing still, nothing happening opening fills the novel's first ten pages. Seriously? *Ten pages* of nothing happening? The opening of a #1 *New York Times* best-seller? How does Goolrick get away with that?

Goolrick's trick is micro-tension. It's not tension from action or dialogue (there's barely any), but from inside Ralph Truitt, who is massively, multiply conflicted about what he is doing:

So Ralph stood implacable, chest out, oblivious to the cold, hardened to the gossip, his eyes fixed on the train tracks wasting away into the distance. He was hopeful, amazed that he was hoping, hoping that he looked all right, not too old, or too stupid, or too unforgiving. Hoping that the turmoil of his soul, his hopeless solitude, was just for this hour before the snow fell and shut them all in, invisible.

He had meant to be a good man, and he was not a bad man. He had taught himself not to want, after his first wanting and losing. Now he wanted something, and his desire startled and enraged him.

Ralph Truitt's conflicting emotions infuse the novel's opening so completely that Goolrick is able to hold readers spellbound for ten inactive pages. That's the power of interior conflict. Tension can exist, and be felt palpably, where it can't actually be seen if inside the point-of-view character is a seething cauldron. Nothing is "happening," but everything is in flux.

What if you just write? Suppose that trying to hold a deliberate intent in mind as you compose, such as *create tension here*, gives you a headache? If you are a wholly organic and intuitive writer, thinking about an effect is antithetical to achieving it. There's nothing wrong with that, yet realize that when an electric current isn't running through the words on a page, then no lights go on in readers' minds. The story remains dark and invisible.

Organic writers may be better off trying not to generate tension as they draft, but instead measuring it in review. As you read over what you've written, pay attention to your feelings. Does a passage make you uneasy, wonder, or fear? Are you squirming, anxious, and impatient? Are you unsure what will happen next? Good. You may have micro-tension going. To be sure of that, run it through your critique group; see if they agree.

My friend Robert Olen Butler is the dean of organic writing. His book *From Where You Dream* (2005) is perhaps the bible of the intuitive fiction process. He advises his students as they read their work to monitor the *thrum* of positive effect, and to mark those passages that discordantly *twang*. The first time I heard Bob say that good writing *thrums*, I thought, *Dude, are you kidding me? Thrum?* But the more I thought about it, the more I realized that he and I are talking about the same thing.

In one of his last interviews, John Updike was asked if there was one theme that unified his work. He replied, "I write about the difference between what we want and what is." The space between desire and doubt is where tension resides. Or, to put it in my terms, conflicting or contrasting emotions generate reader uneasiness.

Use it deliberately or let your process bring it about, but however you handle it, be sure that your final result is a snapping, crackling, continuous current of juice that makes the readers' fingertips tingle. When the voltage is high enough, they'll turn the pages. When the voltage is low, they won't. It's that simple.

PLOT LAYERS

As I mentioned, one nearly universal problem with manuscripts is that not enough is happening in the middle. To add events, it's a good idea to add additional problems for your main character to face. I call these plot layers. They can be life issues, inter-personal puzzles, family conflicts, looming decisions, or any nasty nugget that's not easily resolved or overcome.

Jamie's Ford's *Hotel on the Corner of Bitter and Sweet* (mentioned in chapter three) is a straightforward memory novel built around the experience of a Chinese-American man in Seattle, Henry Lee, as he seeks to reconcile his conflicting feelings about his dual heritage and the loss of his childhood love, a Japanese-American girl who was interred during World War II. That's enough story for a novel, but Ford adds two layers to it. One is Henry's testy relationship with his college-aged son, Marty, whose modern thinking and engagement to a Caucasian girl are hard for Henry to accept. Another revolves around Henry's search for a rare jazz record cut by a Seattle street sax player, Sheldon, who befriends Henry as a boy and becomes his lifelong friend.

Now, strictly speaking, Henry's interest in the history of Seattle jazz and his hunt for Sheldon's sole record appearance isn't necessary to the story. Why include it? It adds a period flavor, naturally, and a contrasting minority experience. It gives Henry and his childhood love, Keiko, a shared interest and focus. (At one point they sneak into a nightclub together to hear Sheldon play.) It also ties together past and present. Sheldon is Henry's sole living link to the events of his past. His visits to his dying friend are among the novel's most heart-wrenching scenes. On the last of them he plays for Sheldon his lost solo on the long-sought and legendary record, now found and restored. Talk about symbols! Ask me, it's impossible to imagine Ford's novel without this layer.

Additional plot layers add richness to a story. They also add opportunities to deepen characters and weave their world and experience into a whole picture that's lifelike and resonant. For that effect to work, layers must intersect with each other. In practical terms that means giving secondary characters things to do in more than one realm of the story and allowing settings to host multiple events.

Think of minor characters as Shakespearean-era actors who play more than one role. Imagine that settings are like event spaces for hire.

Multiple point-of-view novels might seem to automatically create a larger-scale and more active story, but that expansive effect depends on each character having a complete story of her own. If so, how do you weight the different storylines? Who gets the most page time? How many scenes should each point of view have?

Deconstruct out-of-category novels and you'll see that while many points of view are possible, it takes only three to give a novel a "big book" feel. Typically, the main character gets something like 40–50 percent of the scenes. The second lead character gets 20–25 percent of the scenes, and a third character a little less. There's no formula, naturally, but breakdowns show that while protagonists require the most room, other characters also get plenty.

Usually.

Pamela Morsi is a best-selling author of Texas chili-hot women's fiction. Her novel *Red's Hot Honky-Tonk Bar* (2009) is about a fiercely independent forty-six-year-old music bar owner in San Antonio, Red Cullens, who unexpectedly must take in her two grandchildren when her daughter, deployed in Afghanistan, cannot get home as soon as expected and the kids' current caretaker, their other grandmother, has a stroke. The transformation of this tattooed honky-tonk spitfire to PTA mother makes for some hilarious fun. What gives it high impact, though, is the breadth of the story.

Red's Hot Honky-Tonk Bar has only two points of view: Red, plus her granddaughter Olivia, who sends fifteen e-mails to her absent mother. Wait, just one main point of view? How does Morsi manage to give this simple-sounding story a big book feel? She does it first of all by giving Red three plot layers: her sudden status as grandmother, the romance she's resisting with a younger fiddle player, and her struggle to save her bar as San Antonio's downtown development spreads. There are sub-plots, as well, involving the fiddle player (Cam), the kids, a cranky neighbor in Red's new neighborhood, PTA politics, a restaurant romance, and more. Back story secrets are revealed by both Cam and Red.

There's a mother-daughter reconciliation to work out as well, and of course there are the matters of Red's surrender to romance and her need to make peace with the mistakes she's made. All this is done in thirty-four chapters and fifteen e-mails; in other words, big-book feel isn't about brute length and piling on points of view. Even a lean novel (Morsi's is only 350 pages) can still feel big, and have high impact, when stuffed with inner struggles, dramatic events, and active secondary characters.

When do you have too much story? You don't. Trust me, you don't. You may have a manuscript that's too long, but that's a different issue. In that instance, choices must be made. A plot layer can shrink, its scenes cut and their business folded in elsewhere.

If you have difficulty deciding what to let go, let your protagonist be your guide. Your novel is primarily her story.

PAST AND PRESENT STORIES

What if you are unfolding two stories simultaneously, one in the present, the other in the past? Many great novels have followed this pattern, but many manuscripts fail in the attempt. It's best to think of both past and present as novels (or maybe novellas) unto themselves. Could each stand alone in a volume of its own?

Another common manuscript flaw is failing to get two storylines quickly connected. This is especially true when the entire present-day problem is unlocking a secret in the past. Why does it matter? What possible stakes could be high enough to make a revelation from the past one of high consequence in the present? Why is an old mystery worth a whole lot more than a footnote?

Kate Morton's *The Forgotten Garden* (mentioned in chapter four) is a past-present story that unfolds a complex mystery surrounding the arrival of an unaccompanied little girl on an ocean liner in Australia in 1913. Who put her on the ship? The only clue is her white suitcase, which contains a book of dark fairy tales written by a powerful but little-known author named Eliza Makepeace. (Several of these superb tales are included in the novel.) The girl is raised by a kindly Australian couple, who name her Nell.

The mystery of Nell's origins is played out from three points of view: 1) Nell herself, who at age twenty-one learns she was abandoned; 2) Nell's granddaughter, Cassandra, who after her grandmother's death in 2005 inherits a cottage in Cornwall about which she knows nothing; 3) Eliza Makepeace, known to Nell only as The Authoress. The three interwoven narrative lines shuffle in non-linear fashion; indeed the novel's first twin events are Nell's arrival in Australia as a girl and her death many years later.

Morton's ambitious strategy carries many risks, not least of which is confusion for the reader. Morton, however, provides a grounding framework story in Cassandra, whose pursuit of the truth about her grandmother is related in a strictly linear chronology. Cassandra is the detective figure. Slowly she pieces together the story of her grandmother, The Authoress, and the walled-off, "forgotten" garden next to the secret-packed cliffside cottage in Cornwall, which Nell purchased on her one trip back to England in 1975.

Meanwhile, in another story strand, Nell herself pieces together parts of her past, especially on her 1975 journey to the UK. She's unable to return to her investigation, though, because her young granddaughter, Cassandra, is abruptly left in her care (a parallel—see chapter seven). The third strand follows Eliza Makepeace, her urchin beginnings in Edwardian London, childhood on the unhappy Mountrachet family estate with its frightening hedge maze (a symbol—see chapter seven), her devotion to her sickly cousin Rose, her writing, its Freudian psychological roots and, finally, the dangerous and shame-laden sacrifice she makes for her beloved cousin.

The Forgotten Garden is chock-full of messy secrets, strong (if sick) antagonists, forbidden love, family power struggles, and murder. The parallels are rich, the reversals sharp, and the quantity of symbols vast: ships, sketches, walls, thorns, spy holes, X-rays, the hedge maze, the walled-off garden, and many more.

The novel is overloaded, but what keeps it from becoming a chaotic hodgepodge is the firm foundation that Morton puts under it all. The whole story, if continuously told, is pretty nasty but easy to follow. Eliza knows the whole truth but meets a tragic end, leaving Nell literally adrift. Enough clues and witnesses are left, by design, so that Cassandra is later able to find the truth. Cassandra is the anchor character whose action is strictly chronological and who serves as a proxy for the curious reader.

Additionally, Morton immediately gets her storylines connected. She helps herself do that with the novel's non-chronological pattern. Nell's bizarre arrival by ocean liner in 1913 and her death in 2005 are the novel's opening events for a reason: They introduce all the major characters at once (even the mysterious "Authoress") and get them inextricably connected to each other. Each of the three principles have a linked story, it's true, yet each story is nevertheless complete unto itself. And that's the secret: Past and present might come together to make a forest, but first of all they are sturdy trees that stand alone.

AMAZING ENDINGS

Did you ever skim through the final forty or fifty pages of a novel? If you have—I'd be surprised if you haven't—you may have met an ending so suspenseful that you can't wait, but more likely you're speeding toward a conclusion that's all too forgone.

The moral map of most novels makes clear what's good and what's bad. There's an outcome we hope for: a killer caught, a love fulfilled, a disaster averted, a healing achieved, or just everything coming out okay. In most cases that's exactly what happens. Think of it as low suspense or formula writing. The ending is no surprise because the author has set up the story so that the main character will certainly succeed. In other words, the ending lacks drama because the middle of the novel pulls its punches.

Whether it's an outer problem or an inner journey or both, the foundation of a great ending is laid by digging holes as deeply as possible in the middle. Indeed, the surest way to keep readers *unsure* is to let your main character actually fail. Exhaust every option, block every path, alienate every ally, and defeat your protagonist both in fact and in spirit. When every possibility is gone and hope is extinguished, amazingly readers won't give up. They'll be intrigued.

After all, they can see that there are twenty or thirty more pages to go.

Can an ending have been more eagerly anticipated than the final volume of J. K. Rowling's Harry Potter series, *Harry Potter and the Deathly*

Hallows (2007)? In this volume, Harry must finally face up to his fate: He, and only he, can kill the utterly evil wizard Voldemort, who killed Harry's own parents and is well on his way to subjugating all non-magical Muggles (us) and fulfilling his desire to live forever.

Voldemort has split his soul into seven pieces, which are contained in seven magical receptacles called Horcruxes. To vanquish Voldemort, Harry and his friends Hermione and Ron must not only find the Horcruxes but figure out how to destroy them. This isn't easy. Many friends die along the way. Worse, Harry discovers that the father figure in his life, Dumbledore, the (mostly dead) headmaster of Hogwarts, is a man he didn't really know. In his youth Dumbledore espoused the same philosophy as Voldemort, the fascistic "right to rule" Muggles. The discovery is devastating:

> "Harry, I'm sorry, but I think the reason you're so angry is that Dumbledore never told you any of this himself."
>
> "Maybe I am!" Harry bellowed, and he flung his arms over his head, hardly knowing whether he was trying to hold in his anger or protect himself from the weight of his own disillusionment. "Look at what he asked from me, Hermione! Risk your life, Harry! And again! And again! And don't expect me to explain everything, just trust me blindly, trust me that I know what I'm doing, trust me even though I don't trust you! Never the whole truth! Never!"
>
> His voice cracked with the strain, and they stood looking at each other in the whiteness and the emptiness, and Harry felt they were as insignificant as insects beneath the wide sky.
>
> "He loved you," Hermione whispered. "I know he loved you."
>
> Harry dropped his arms.
>
> "I don't know who he loved, Hermione, but it was never me. This isn't love, the mess he's left me in."

Pretty heavy stuff for a young adult novel, don't you think? It gets worse. In the novel's climactic sequence, Harry learns that the final Horcrux is actually himself. To finally and completely destroy Voldemort, Harry too must die. Only just turned seventeen, he must make the supreme sacrifice. There's no out. Even the three-part magical protection against death, the Deathly Hallows of the title, won't save him. There's a magic wand that will, but before Rowling gives him this gimmick she makes Harry die. Every possibility is gone. Every hope is extinguished.

It's a hell of an ending.

Except, of course, it's not the end. Rowling must untwist a few knots, and dump in quite a few pages of explanatory dialogue, but at the last she gets Harry out of his death sentence. Love, the sacrifices of Harry's parents and of Dumbledore too, allow Harry to survive and extinguish Voldemort once and for all.

The other component of amazing endings is bringing about a change in a protagonist that hitherto has felt impossible. This transformative power will be more effective if the need to change grows more urgent even as it becomes less likely.

It's hard to torment characters; even harder when their problems are their own fault. Readers might give up. But ask yourself, do you give up on the people you love? Of course not. If your readers are bonded to a character because that character has qualities that allow readers to care, your readers won't give up either.

Like you, they'll live in hope . . . and in suspense about your final chapters.

THE FOURTH LEVEL

So far in this chapter we've been focusing on the mechanics of novel construction: plot, scene, and micro-tension. But there's a fourth level on which novels can work. Great ones do, anyway. It's the level of art; meaning the way in which the author unfolds his intentions. An artless novel throws its point in with a splash, either right away or at the end. An artful novel leads the reader this way and that, making the reader guess, ponder, and work at what this story means.

Mystery writers mislead readers with clues, creating so-called *red herrings* that send the suspicions of readers off in various directions. Going-home-to-heal novels do something similar. They plant a secret or emotional mystery, then play out its discovery. Those are fine plot patterns, but too often they depend on simple delay. Have you ever grown impatient with such a novel? If you have, then you've seen what I mean. Mere delay is not strong.

Obfuscation isn't the point, nor am I recommending that you embrace the avoidant message of experimental fiction. Such stuff can be effective, of course, and had its era back in the 1960s and 1970s. B. S. Johnson and, more familiarly, John Fowles wrote novels that undermined the contract between author and reader. *The Magus* (1966) and the slyly experimental romance *The French Lieutenant's Woman* (1969) finally left their meanings up to the reader. More recent experiments with hypertext, multimedia, and interactive fiction are in truth more akin to games, which are by nature morally neutral and therefore unsatisfying as stories.

21ˢᵗ century fiction, by contrast, takes a strong stand. But when it's artful, that stand isn't easily and immediately apparent. It plays games with readers' heads, explaining why *unreliable narrators* are so popular. Gimmicks aren't needed, though. It's possible to lead your readers on a merry, moral dance simply on purpose.

To do that requires that you give yourself ultimate control of your story. It takes confidence. It demands that your point be one that you're willing to withhold. You must be willing to mislead your readers, not with dark and hopeless characters whom you will—*surprise!*—redeem after a dreary and depressing slog of a story, but with a lively game of guessing what's right and wrong.

The easiest way to do that is to let your protagonist do something that's actually wrong. Another strategy is to let your protagonist do something good that turns out badly. Or build a moral dilemma: a difficult choice between two rights or two wrongs.

Pause during your process and ask, "What do I want my reader, at this point, to be thinking?" You can influence that thinking to your design. You may worry that you're confounding readers, turning them off, but if you've grounded them strongly that won't happen. The bond you've built with your protagonist will pull them through. The rich story world you've constructed will continue to fascinate. If nothing else, the micro-tension that infuses your novel will make it impossible for them to stop turning pages.

Robert Goolrick's *A Reliable Wife* is a simple story. Reclusive businessman Ralph Truitt advertises for, and marries, a "reliable wife," Catherine Land, whom he met via correspondence; except that she's not reliable at all, but rather a con artist who plans to poison him slowly with arsenic. There's no mystery to this. Catherine's true nature and plan are made known to the reader in the novel's second chapter. And poison him she does. So where is there for the story to go? Where's the suspense when we know exactly what will happen?

The suspense in the story, and Goolrick's manipulation of his readers' expectations, arises from the uncertainty of whether Catherine will go through with her plan. At first there's no question that she will. Even as she arrives in a private train car this is apparent:

> Catherine Land sat in front of the mirror, unbecoming all that she had become. The years had hardened her beyond mercy.
> I'm the kind of woman who wants to know the end of the story, she thought, staring at her face in the jostling mirror. I want to know how it's all going to end before it even starts.

But is that true? Look at that passage again, especially the first line: ". . . unbecoming all that she had become." Now, Catherine is changing her costume, we discover, from a lavish dress to a shabby one that befits her false front. Is that all that Goolrick means? As the novel unfolds Goolrick plants doubts. A possible transformation is foreshadowed in a carriage accident that, literally, turns Catherine over. She becomes fascinated with the palazzo, long abandoned, that Truitt built for his dead Italian wife. She affirms her dark intentions, but too emphatically. They marry. She enjoys making love with Truitt. She delays the poison.

At this point we have ample reason to wonder if Catherine might change. No sooner does Goolrick provoke that idea than he reverses it. Truitt tells Catherine that he has an estranged, ne'er-do-well son whom he has tracked down via a detective, who reports that the son is a lost cause. But Truitt wants to reconcile. He asks Catherine to go to St. Louis, meet with the detective and speak with his dissolute, opium-addicted, piano-playing son. What Truitt doesn't know, and we learn, is that Catherine already knows this son, Tony Moretti. They are lovers and the plan to poison Truitt is one they hatched together. Ah. Our expectations swing.

Catherine commences the poisoning. Truitt suffers in agony. Tony Moretti arrives. The outcome of the story looks certain, and justified. Moretti says that his father beat his mother to death. However, in a key moment of honesty, Truitt confesses to Catherine the truth: When his wife admitted she'd used him he cast her out. She died of tuberculosis in a charity hospital. Catherine is moved by his confession; his sins are understandable and, really, so much less then hers. She decides that Truitt is enough for her. She breaks it off with Moretti and discontinues the poison. She is pregnant with Truitt's child. Goolrick has tricked us again, firmly in control of our thinking.

It's not the last time that Goolrick plays with our belief about his novel's outcome, either. In its violent conclusion, Moretti tries to rape Catherine, she stabs him, father and son struggle, and the fight moves outside in the bitter Wisconsin winter where Moretti falls through ice and drowns in a pond. Following the son's funeral Truitt reveals to Catherine that he's known all along her true nature and plans. The detective told him in a letter.

Surely this will reverse things again? No. In a triple Lutz on the final page, Truitt says he burned the letter: "It's private and it means nothing." We realize that he endured the poison knowingly. Really? Why? There can only be one reason: Truitt has found the life and love he wanted, however flawed. And Catherine has, too. The novel's final lines make clear they will go on. This might strike you as improbable after all that's gone down, but Goolrick challenges us to disagree with him in his brash final line:

Such things happen.

With your reader in your grip, you can do anything. It's primary to make your audience feel something as you unfold your story; even higher impact is achieved when you make them think. But think what? Ah. You must think first. Decide what it is that you're saying through your novel, then send messages that mislead. When your readers (temporarily) believe something that you're not (ultimately) saying, you're writing fiction at the level of art.

Are you a novelist crafty and secure enough to play mind games with your readers? It's a strength you can build. It begins with two intentions: first, the point or purpose of your novel; second, the aim of keeping your readers from too quickly or easily seeing what that is. Call it *withholding*, if that helps. Conceptualize it as *misdirection*, if you like. However you think of it, make your readers think. It's the ultimate in high impact.

⟶ 21ˢᵀ CENTURY TOOLS ⟵

INHERENT CONFLICT

- In your story, what's the problem that's tough to solve? Make it impossible to solve.
- Which characters in your story are set against each other? Work until their conflicts cannot possibly be settled.
- Divide your cast into opposing camps, one being pro-protagonist. What grievances or injustices run so deep that they have no choice but to remain at war?
- In the world of your story, what ideas are in opposition? Build them until they represent two (or more) irreconcilable philosophies.

GUT EMOTIONAL APPEAL

- What's the worst turn of events for your protagonist? What's the personal cost of this disaster? Make that element primary to her happiness.
- What's the most dramatic reversal in your story? Find three new ways to deepen this calamity.
- Who can betray your protagonist? What's the worst way in which that can be done?
- Your protagonist's worst mistake is—? For whom is that error unforgiveable? Destroy that relationship, but then heal it with forgiveness.
- What love is forbidden? Make it more impossible. Then make it happen.
- Kill a beloved character. Increase that character's innocence, warmth, spirit, generosity, or wisdom.
- What death, disaster, or misfortune has boxed in your protagonist for life? What concrete reasons keep your protagonist from escaping that grip? Strengthen those. Add to them.

- Who in the story has been cast under a spell? What locks that spell in place, never to be broken? Break it.
- Who can't forget a past wrong? Why not? Move that character to the center of the story.
- Something is wrong in your story world. It's a whirlpool. Who else can be sucked into its vortex, and how?

PLAUSIBLE

- What's your story's most unlikely, improbable event? Write out six reasons why this usually doesn't happen in the real world. Answer those reasons with six explanations why, in this case, it does occur. Add.
- If you're writing a thriller, the unlikely event cited above is the looming threat or disaster. Increase your list to twenty.
- Quick, what's something that can happen to anybody? Don't think. Write it down. How can that happen to your protagonist in the course of the story?
- What's your protagonist's most heroic act? What's one way in which it's something anyone could do? Echo or incorporate that.
- If your story involves magic, the paranormal, a leap of science, slaying monsters, a criminal act, conspiracy, quest, war, or survival . . . what's the small, real-world, garden-variety equivalent? Find two ways to add that mundane, analogous element.
- If your story realistically captures life the way it is, ask, *What utterly outrageous thing does my protagonist secretly long to do?* Do it.

ORIGINAL

- What's one convention of your genre or story type that you have honored in your manuscript? Reverse it. Is that interesting? Keep it.

- What's your protagonist's profession? What's one stereotype of people who do that kind of work? Reverse it.
- What's the main outward and objective problem facing your protagonist? (That is, if your protagonist weren't around, what's the problem someone else would nevertheless have to deal with?) When this problem occurs, it usually looks like what—? Escalate, warp, or twist it in a way that no one expects.
- Where is your story set? Give the place itself a personality trait that is the opposite of what we're used to.

MORE IN THE MIDDLE

- What's your protagonist trying to do? What else can go wrong? Add it. Repeat. Again.
- What's your protagonist trying to do? What's the worst thing that can go wrong? Poor protagonist! Too bad. Make it happen.
- How many things can your protagonist try to solve the problem? Make a list. Make it longer. Let your protagonist try each solution. Make each one fail.
- What does your protagonist want to become? What's getting in the way? Add more blocks. Fold them in.
- What's the last, most desperate thing your protagonist can try or do? Push her into it.
- Drop a bombshell on your protagonist. Scatter the wreckage. List the consequences. Incorporate it all.
- Where's the story going? Close that road. Force a detour.
- When does your protagonist want to explode? How? Light the fuse and stand back. Kaboom!
- Create an impossible choice. Work backwards to deviously box in your protagonist. No cheating. No escape. Whatever he decides, big consequences. Make them bigger.

- Imagine a more fearless writer than you creates an event for your story. What is it? Use it.

STRONG SCENES

- Pick a blah scene in your manuscript. What changes here? Exactly when does that change occur? What would an impartial observer see or hear to make the change impossible to miss? Add or strengthen that. (That is the outer turning point.)
- Ten minutes before the change, how would your protagonist describe the essence of himself? Write it out. Ten minutes after the turning point . . . how does your protagonist see himself now? Write it out. (The change is the scene's inner turning point.)
- Follow the above two prompts for every middle scene.
- What's the outer turning point in your current scene? Make its trigger more dramatic—or less obvious.
- Pick a weak scene. What are three setting details that only your point-of-view character would notice? How does this place feel, or make your character feel? Create a passage of subjective opinion regarding the place itself. Delete all other description.
- Imagine the scene is a person. What mood is it in? How does that mood change following the turning point? Add.
- How does your POV character change in your current scene? Work backwards. Make that change unlikely, a surprise, or impossible.
- In this scene, what does your POV character hope to get? Will he get it or not? What are three things that will misdirect the reader from the actual outcome? Delete as much else as possible.
- The prompt above creates a reversal. Strengthen that turnabout. Make one outcome utterly certain. Make the actual outcome the exact opposite.
- Find a dialogue passage. Strip it down. Take out all attributives ("he said," "she said"). Take out all incidental action. Take out all exposi-

tion. Reduce each thing said to ten words or less until the dialogue fires quickly back and forth, rat-a-tat.

- Take a passage of exposition in this scene and turn it into dialogue.
- Pick a blah middle scene. Summarize what happens in a paragraph. Reduce that to one line. Can you substitute that for the scene?
- Pick a scene where nothing overtly happens or changes. Rewrite it using only actions: no dialogue, no exposition. What do we see? Make us see more. Now add the results.
- Pick a scene of high action. Rewrite it using only exposition; that is, internal thoughts and feelings. How many different emotions does your character feel? In the actual scene cut the action in half. Add the most unusual feelings.
- In your current scene, what's the best zinger line? Structure the scene to make that the last line.
- In your current scene, cut 100 words. You have five minutes. Fail? Cut 200 words.

MICRO-TENSION

- Pick a passage of dialogue. Strip it down. Increase hostility between the speakers. It can be friendly ribbing, worried questioning, polite disagreement, snide derision, veiled threats, open hostility, or any other degree of friction.
- Repeat the prompt above 100 times.
- Pick a passage of action—anything from high violence to a stroll in the park. Freeze the action in a sequence of three to five still snapshots. Select a detail from each frame. For each snapshot record your POV character's precise feelings. Discard obvious emotions. Choose emotions that contrast or conflict. Rewrite the passage.
- Repeat the prompt above 50 times.

- Pick a passage of exposition. List all of your POV character's emotions. List all ideas. Discard what's obvious. Find emotions that conflict. Find ideas at war. Grab what creates unease, uncertainty, fresh worry, new questions, a deeper puzzle, or agonizing dilemma. Rewrite the passage.
- Repeat the prompt above 100 times. (If you are a romance writer, repeat 200 times.)
- Pick a moment when your protagonist is still, simply waiting or doing nothing. Look around. List three setting details that only this character would notice. Detail her emotions. Find those that conflict or surprise her. What's this moment's personal meaning? Write a passage combining snapshot clarity and roiling inner intensity.
- Print out your manuscript. Randomize the pages. Examine each one in isolation. Does it crackle? Are the characters on tiptoe? What question arises that the reader can't answer? What's going badly or wrong for your POV character? How does this page tell the whole story? Revise until the tension level is unbearable.
- Repeat the prompt above for every page. Yes, seriously.

PLOT LAYERS

- What's a stage-of-life problem your protagonist would be facing at this time, even if the events of the story weren't happening? Add it.
- Deepen that problem. List most people's normal, dependable solutions. Decide why in this case each one won't work. Turn each failure into a scene.
- Create echoes: Who else can have this problem, or the opposite problem? Create a parallel event from this layer in another layer. When can an event in this layer overlap (occur at the same time as) a main storyline event?

- What's a third not-easy-to-solve problem your protagonist could face, the kind of thing that could trouble anyone? Deepen it. Take away solutions. Add.
- Pick a secondary character. If this character had a volume of his own, what would it be about? What would his main problem or conflict be? Complicate it in four ways. Add.
- Weave the layers and storylines: What secondary character can play a role in the main plot and another layer? What location can host multiple events? Find as many such connections as you can.

PAST AND PRESENT STORYLINES

- Separate the past and present scenes into two different documents, as if each were a novel standing alone. Is each scene in each document strong? Does each story rise, deepen, and complicate? If not, cut and revise. Weave the documents together again only after you have storylines that work on their own.

MULTI-POV NOVELS

- In a multi-POV novel, collect scenes from each POV into separate documents. Is each scene strong? Is there a complete story told from each POV?

ENDINGS

- What would cause your protagonist to fail? What would signal that defeat? What, in this story, does it mean to lose? Go there.
- What miracle does your protagonist pray for? Make it impossible. Then make it happen.

- Everything comes out okay . . . except for—? What cost has been too great? What decision will always feel wrong? What failure along the way darkens the final success?
- How do things come out better than imagined? What's an unexpected gift or unforeseen joy at the end?

THE FOURTH LEVEL

- The "onion layer" effect: What's the big secret you're keeping from the reader? Invent two other secrets to reveal earlier.
- Pick a character about whom you want your readers to have doubts. Keep them guessing. Pick four points in your story to swing your readers' thinking. Make those events stronger, each time digging the readers' doubts deeper.
- What's the ultimate point of your novel: the message, meaning, or whatever you want readers to see? Challenge your own wisdom. List all the arguments against it. Include those in your story. Assign each objection to a character.
- For each character who represents an outlook that opposes yours, find one way in which each will demonstrate the validity of her belief.

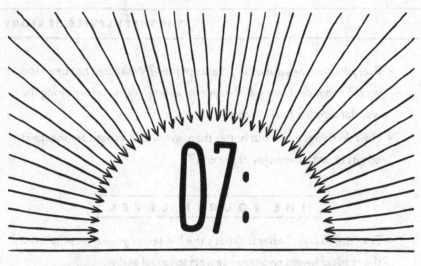

07:

BEAUTIFULLY WRITTEN

You can tell publishing professionals by the questions they ask. Describe your novel to an agent or editor and their first question usually is, "Who's your publisher?" It's like asking, "Where are you from?" The answer doesn't really matter, it's just a quick way to tag and feel at ease with someone. Then you move on.

Publishing pros also tend to discuss novels in shorthand. If you were to eavesdrop in the International Rights Centre at the London Book Fair, say, the comment you'd probably most often hear as novels are pitched is, "It's beautifully written," followed by, "of course."

Beautifully written. What a nice thing to hear, even more so when it's your novel that's being praised.

For me, beautifully written has come to mean not just a nice extra (when you get it), but a critical component of high-impact fiction. Commercial storytellers may scoff. Um, have you looked at the best-seller list? Yes, I have. There's plenty of plain prose to be found there. But look closer. Novels that have run for a year or more on the lists are rarely just slick genre fare. It's fiction that is both powerfully plotted and beautifully written.

Commercial storytellers, and even many literary novelists, take that term to mean imagery that is deft, observant, and fresh. No question, that's a good thing. But beautifully written isn't just about imagery. Indeed, one needn't have a descriptive eye at all to create high impact on the page. High impact, in turn, doesn't mean just high sales. It means moving readers' hearts, changing their ideas, and even rocking their worlds.

What does that? Beautiful writing is more than pretty prose. It creates resonance in readers' minds with parallels, reversals, and symbols. It conjures a story world that is unique, highly detailed, and brought alive by the characters who dwell there. It offers moments of breath-catching surprise, heart-gripping insight, revelation, and self-understanding. It engages the reader's mind with an urgent point, which we might call *theme*.

Beautiful writing also illuminates a story's social world, its era, the passage of time, the story's larger meaning, and even the profound puzzles of existence such as the question of destiny and man's relationship to the gods. When a novel's grasp is sure and its ambition is vast, then it is beautifully written.

PARALLELS, REVERSALS, AND SYMBOLS

My four-year-old son likes to play a connect-the-dots game on my iPhone. When the numbers or letters are linked up, there appears a picture of a dinosaur, kangaroo, or penguin. Connect dots in your novel and there will be an association in your readers' minds too. *Ding!* This and that and the other thing link up. There's a deeper and hidden meaning that suddenly is revealed.

High school English teachers have long understood the power of associations. Remember writing a term paper on symbols in *The Scarlet Letter*? Much as I hate to admit it, those English teachers were on to something. There's power in association. The sense of meaning conveyed through parallels, reversals, and symbols isn't something one can always explain. The suggestion made by such devices is by its nature fleeting and mysterious. But it's there.

Parallels associate two things by their similar nature or pattern. They can be constructed in many ways. Plot threads can align and mirror. Story events can repeat in analogous ways. Characters can perform comparable actions. The inner journeys in your story can be multi-part harmony, or variations on a theme.

Kathryn Stockett's *The Help* (discussed in chapter five) is shot through with parallels. Its heroine, recent college grad "Skeeter" Phelan, dreams of being a writer, but the best she can do is compile an anonymous column of household tips for the local paper. See the ironic parallel? Skeeter is white, giving out cleaning advice, when the real experts are the novel's black maids.

Those maids are the object of a racist piece of law that one of Skeeter's friends, Junior League leader Hilly Holbrook, is trying to get passed: the "Home Help Sanitation Initiative," which will require homeowners to construct separate bathrooms outside for their black help. Bathrooms and elimination are thereafter neatly paralleled as maid Aibileen Clark potty trains the toddler of another Junior Leaguer, Elizabeth Leefolt. The child, Mae Mobley, has none of the prejudices of her mother, at one point in her potty training insisting that Aibileen use her toilet first.

That's not all. At another point, Skeeter must grovel, dissemble, and lie to get out of trouble, getting a taste of what the help endure. At the story's conclusion, human waste comes back for a final ironic parallel when it emerges that several of the Jackson society ladies have been served, and have eaten, pie with small amounts of feces baked in. Delicious . . . in a literary way, I mean. The parallels in *The Help* may be blunt, but do you mind them? Five million readers didn't, nor did film producer Chris Columbus, hundreds of reviewers and award committees, or for that matter anyone else. The parallels are part of what gives *The Help* high impact.

Ever had a change of fortune? Did you see it coming? Probably not. Windfalls are like that. Losses, too. We're taken by surprise. Suddenly we're hurtling in the wrong direction down the highway. Assumptions flip over. The world spins upside down. Coins fall out of our pockets, or into them. We're weightless: falling, or rising, and unsure of when or where we'll land.

Reversals have that effect on your readers. It's the stomach-dropping feeling as the roller coaster car tops the highest rise; the sharp intake of breath before the screaming plunge. Rational thought is suspended. Existence itself shrinks to a single second. In that frozen moment anything is possible, yet nothing is under control. Your characters, and your readers, are in the hands of a maniacal god, who in this instance is you, the storyteller.

To create that effect in your fiction you've first got to construct the roller coaster rise. Crank your characters up, up, up, then fling them into the blue. Will they fly or crash? That's up to you. Either way, there's going to be a radical change of direction—and a breathless, exhilarating moment in your story.

Do you recall the wedding of Kate Middleton and Prince William, heir to the British throne? Remember the mystery surrounding her dress? Months of speculation preceded the event. Finally, the day arrived and the dress was revealed. TV commentators quickly began to deconstruct it as the bride slowly processed down the aisle of Westminster Abbey. Many remarked that it paid homage to the wedding dress of Grace Kelly, another commoner who became a princess. It affirmed that every girl is a princess inside.

Common and obvious symbols are lame: dove, eagle, rose, sunrise, winter, lightning. Others are so obtuse that they are eternal fodder for term papers: albatross, white whale, the Valley of Ashes. The strongest symbols evoke emotions and ideas. Characters themselves can be symbolic. Think *Animal Farm* or *Lord of the Flies*.

Even novels of deliberately commercial intent can add impact with symbols. Susan Wiggs is a best-selling, multiple-award-winning author of more than forty works of romance and women's fiction, many of which involve returning to a childhood place, healing, and love. *Just Breathe* (2008) is about Sarah Moon, an underground cartoonist from California who, as the novel opens, is married to a Chicago real estate developer. For a year her husband has been fighting cancer while she tries (with his frozen sperm) to get pregnant through artificial insemination. Twelve fertility procedures have failed. Sarah is discouraged. One wintery Chicago day, she drives to one of her husband's developments, bringing him his favorite pizza for lunch. There, in a half-finished house, she finds him lunching, as it were, on another woman.

Devastated, Sarah heads home to the California coast to find love with a high school hero who never left. But her anger gets in the way. Her new love, fireman Will Bonner, advises her to get mad, throw things. Halfway through the novel she phones her not-yet-ex-husband to say that, ironically, she is pregnant after all. When her husband Jack is a jerk about the news, Sarah draws his face (she's a cartoonist) on a dozen eggs in a carton and drives to the shore:

> She brought the sack of groceries to the overlook, took out an egg with Jack's face on it and let fly. The egg soared high in a perfect arc into the sky. Then it plummeted to the rocks below and the waves surged in to carry the mess out to sea.
>
> She picked up another and threw it. *Take that. And that.* One after another, she hurled the eggs, and when she ran out, she moved on to the lemons and oranges and potatoes. With every throw, the poison ebbed as though sucked out to sea.
>
> Minutes later, the sack was empty. Her shoulders ached, her arm muscles felt slack and fatigued and her mind was quiet.
>
> Just as Will had promised.

Get it? Twelve failed inseminations, twelve eggs tossed away . . . it's a symbol. Pretty hard to miss, you'd think, though students at a workshop I was privileged to teach with Wiggs were surprised when I pointed it out. Readers aren't always aware of symbols, but the associations they create worm their way in even so. They carry meaning.

Symbols don't need to be large and recurring, either. They can be here and gone, like flash mobs. In the workshop I just mentioned, I highlighted a number of small symbols in the opening scene of *Just Breathe*. As Sarah brings her unfaithful husband a pizza, the weather is bad. Her husband is supposedly impotent from the chemo; significantly, Sarah's car is out of windshield fluid—it won't squirt. She also discovers Jack with another woman in an unfinished house. I asked Wiggs in the workshop whether these symbols were put in deliberately or if they were accidental.

They're deliberate, she said, adding, "You missed about six more!" Her heroine is "hungry" for a child; wouldn't you know, it's lunchtime. She gets "stuck" in traffic. She brings her husband a Coke with "extra ice." Leaving the scene, her car skids in mud. She knocks over a mailbox. Those are all flash symbols. They go by largely unnoticed but subconsciously add to the scene depth by association.

As you create parallels, reversals, and symbols using the prompts at the end of this chapter, do they strike you as ridiculously overt? Are you worried that you're overdoing them?

Don't be. In virtually all manuscripts symbols and other associative devices are not overused but rather are underused, if they're used at all. It's hard to overdo them unless you're being horribly obvious with symbols such as lightning bolts. Parallels and reversals can connect dots hundreds of pages apart, too. It's amazing how the unconscious minds of readers not only pick up what their conscious minds miss, but how they crave the meaning you plant with associative devices.

STORY WORLD

Here's a writing craft tool that you can remove from your toolbox and throw away: description. It's the stuff that most readers skim. Even when deftly done using the five senses it's a lead weight. It isn't needed anymore. In the jet-packed 21ˢᵗ century it's a horse carriage.

What has replaced description is a character's experience of her story world. Call it *point-of-view description* if you like, but I believe it's more than conveying how things look, sound, smell, feel, and taste. It's a total immersion in every dimension of what occurs. Some of what we want to feel in a novel is intangible: mood, atmosphere, a defined moment. In intimate third-person point of view, everything is subjective. (In first-person POV, that's inescapably true.) No person, place, or thing actually has objective qualities; maybe in science, but not in fiction.

High impact happens when we take in another's way of thinking and feeling. *I get it! I understand now!* Those are more powerful reactions to provoke in readers than a feather-light recognition of how something looks. To create that effect means writing entirely from inside the skin of your characters. It's not just the objects they observe, but the totality of their perceptions.

As human beings we perceive rubber handles, popping corks, crème centers, lavender lotion, and autumn leaves as real. But just as solid to us are snotty attitudes, inconvenient lust, spade flushes, political lies, steely beauty, hometown support, big-city zeal, coffee intoxication, bizarre fashion moments, cell-phone lobotomies, road rage, pathetic dreams, and a thousand other things that aren't corporeal. To capture what makes a character grounded, for instance, it isn't enough for them to own a home. We need to see it on Christmas morning and when the roof collapses.

Hollywood novels are prone to superficial gloss, an excess of glitz and glitter. There's another side to Hollywood, though, the gritty reality of the day-to-day movie business. This is the side brought to life in Daniel Depp's *Loser's Town* (2009), a novel about ex-stuntman turned detective David Spandau, who is hired to help a rising young male star who's being blackmailed; not for money, interestingly, but for a break in the business.

Toward the novel's beginning, Spandau drives across L.A. to meet the star to see if they have the right chemistry. Travel scenes are frequently low-tension filler, but Depp handles the drive with more than a descriptive eye:

> Spandau smoked, and thought the city gliding past was like an overexposed film, too much light, all depth burned away and sacrificed. All concrete and asphalt, a thousand square miles of man-made griddle on which to fry for our sins. Then you turn a corner and there's a burst of crimson bougainvillea redeeming an otherwise ugly chunk of concrete building. Or a line of tall palm trees, still majestic and refusing to die, stubbornly sprouting green at the tops of thick dying stalks, guarding a side street of bungalows constructed at a time when L.A. was still the Land of Milk and Honey. If you squinted hard, you could imagine what brought them here, all those people. There was a beauty still there, sometimes, beneath all the corruption, like in the face of an actress long past her prime, when the outline of an old loveliness can still be glimpsed through the desperate layers of pancake and eyeliner. Spandau could never figure out why he stayed, what kept bringing him back to L.A., until a drunken conversation he'd had in Nevada with a cowboy who'd fallen in love with a middle-aged whore. It was true, said the cowboy, that she was old and greedy and had no morals to speak of. But sometimes when she slept she had the face of a young girl, and it was this young girl the cowboy kept falling in love with, over and over. And also, added the cowboy, she had tricks that could make you the happiest man alive when she was in the mood.
>
> He was thinking again of leaving Los Angeles.

That's some beautiful writing, to be sure, and some striking details to bring L.A. visually alive. But what is it that keeps this passage from being more than just description? Right, it's Spandau's feelings. He's conflicted. He loves Los Angeles and he hates it; hates it and loves it with a ferocity that's positively Biblical. (Look again at the language.) His view of Los Angeles isn't objective: He's immersed in it, trapped by it, thrilled by it, disgusted by it, longing to leave and unable to go.

In other words, Depp (who has plenty of L.A. experience himself; he's a screenwriter and brother of a famous actor) is using the totality of Spandau's experience to make this not just a place, but a personal world. What about the world of your story? Does your protagonist merely inhabit it, reporting its details dryly, or is she passionately engaged, afraid, offended, in love and altogether opinionated about it? Why not? Your protagonist's feelings are the lightning bolts that animate the monster and make it live.

SURPRISE

Do you like surprise parties? Watch videos of them and the reactions are frequently the same. As the victim enters there's a loud, "Surprise!" The victim looks shocked. Her hands fly to her face. Her head shakes, "No!"

Resistance and denial is a natural response. After all, a surprise means an unexpected and involuntary change of plans. It's inconvenient. But soon enough the party is underway. Even the victim is having a great time. Everyone's happy that the surprise was planned.

Surprises in your stories can be planned too, but creating them is likely to leave you feeling victimized. It's a change of plans. It's inconvenient. To make the party fun is going to take a lot of work. You'll have to organize the big moment even while keeping it a big secret. But hey, in the end the party will rock.

Often story surprises are not much of a jolt. Did you ever see a plot turn coming miles away? The fault may lie in poor concealment but more likely the error is that the "turn" is something we expect. Events that unfold like they're supposed to cannot surprise.

What if you're an organic sort of writer, one for whom "planning" is synonymous with "spoiling"? Probably you hope to surprise your readers once in a while. When you do, the muse has smiled.

Lightning-strike revelations about your characters, sudden insights, *oh-my-God-where-did-that-come-from?* . . . these are wonderful gifts from the muse, but why not summon those cranky muses and demand your due? Try it. Think about your main character. What's she been keeping from you? What about him would upset his friends? Guess what? Make it part of the story.

In other words, strange as it sounds, plan to surprise yourself. Does that sound ridiculous? It isn't. The fact is that everything that your conscious mind has yet to discover about your characters and story is already fully formed in your unconscious mind. It's all been there since the moment the first hint of the story surfaced. Your rational brain has just been blocking access.

Surprising yourself is nothing more than removing the barriers between you and your story. Call it flow, the groove, the zone, or whatever you like. Just get there. It's a state you've already experienced, when everything easily pours out, all cylinders are firing, confidence is rocketing, time is meaningless, and the blank screen stretches ahead like a highway with no speed limit. Writing at peak performance level can become a habit.

Writing euphoria is a common experience for fiction writers, but it's not by itself the measure of success. A good writing day is one in which you see on the page something you didn't expect, something that makes you amazed. It might scare you, but that's okay. Fear is your friend. It's a gauge. You want to be in the red zone. That means that your readers' emotions will be, too.

However you manage to work surprises, shake up your idea of your story. That's fearful. It's messy. It takes extra effort. But it's worth doing.

A SENSE OF SELF

Know thyself. That advice was one of three dictums inscribed in the Temple of Apollo at Delphi, but really it's a prime directive. What subject is more absorbing than ourselves? Discovering who we are is a primary preoccupation of early adulthood. Life review, the affirmation of what our lives have meant, is a critical task of old age. In between is a journey in which our self-understanding grows insight by insight, day by day.

In our search for self-understanding we look for guides. Everything from Oprah to self-help books takes advantage of this need. We talk to therapists. We confide in friends. We argue with God. Vacations, meditation, yoga, retreats, the Dali Lama, and Deepak Chopra give us opportunities to reflect. Philosophy provides a framework. Religions put us in perspective to God. The best insights we get into ourselves come at serendipitous moments: an observation of a friend, a reflection in a window, the sudden realization of what matters most when we're wheeled into surgery.

The British fascination with royals and the American obsession with celebrities are driven, I believe, by the need to have others against whom we can measure our conduct, our values, and our progress. The protagonists in fiction serve a similar purpose. We look to them as models. What we want from them is not just entertaining stories, but examples of how we may feel, see the world, conduct ourselves, grow, and change. We admire them, learn from them, celebrate them, and return to them over and over for comfort and inspiration. They're not termed *heroes* and *heroines* for nothing.

At the beginning of your novel, how does your protagonist understand himself? Who is he? What defines him? What code or rules guide him? What assumptions does he take as givens? What's home base? Who's on his side? In whose love is he secure? Who else does he know as well as he knows himself? What's his snapshot take on money, prayer, pop music, abstract art, minivans, modern dance, fourth-down passes, bespoke suits, raw food, blended whiskey, or anything else that demands an opinion?

At the end of your novel, how has the answer changed to any of the questions above? The difference is a measure of your character's growth. Plant any of that at the beginning, revisit it at the end, and you've got a tangible shift in understanding of self and the world.

The handsome but amoral knight Jaime Lannister in George R. R. Martin's massive fantasy sequence *A Song of Ice and Fire* (mentioned in chapter four) is a character who changes after having his sword hand chopped off. But whom does he change into? In a crypt early in the fourth volume, *A Feast for Crows*, Jaime has a moment of self-understanding:

> Unbidden, his thoughts went to Brienne of Tarth. Stupid stubborn ugly wench. He wondered where she was. Father, give her strength. Almost a prayer . . . but was it the god he was invoking, the Father Above whose towering gilded likeness glimmered in the candlelight across the sept? Or was he praying to the corpse that lay before him? Does it matter? They never listened, either one. The Warrior had been Jaime's god since he was old enough to hold a sword. Older men might be fathers, sons, husbands, but never Jaime Lannister, whose sword was as golden as his hair. He was a warrior, and that was all he would ever be.

We tend to think of gaining self-understanding as empowerment, but sometimes it's letting go. Jaime Lannister is revising his ambitions for himself downward, but it's nevertheless an uplifting release. He is what he is. What of your protagonist? What does he discover himself to be? What about herself must she accept?

Take time to self-assess. Do it with tension, of course. (In the passage above, notice Jaime's appeal to a god, whom he then sourly dismisses as deaf.) Such a passage may not move the plot, but it will advance the arc of your character's growth. It's a higher human need that, done effectively, timed well, will touch your readers with its beauty.

THE BIG PICTURE

One of my favorite workshop prompts is this one: Define the main problem facing your protagonist. What's the larger problem of which this is but a dimension? What's the problem that can never be solved?

Novelists like to think of themselves as beholders of the big picture, but almost never do I read a manuscript that makes me think about timeless questions or eternal mysteries. Indeed, the burning issues of the slush pile these days seem to be whether the undead can really get drunk and where they can send their dry cleaning. (Blood stains are hard to get out, you see.)

All stories take place in a social context. Even if your protagonist is a loner, there's a community around him. If your protagonist is on the run, that's especially true: He's running not only from the law or bad boys but what those groups represent.

What is it you want to show readers about your story's social world? What nuances might they miss? What values do they not see? Which stereotypes are dead on and which are dead wrong? What secrets does this place hide? What tragedies does it memorialize? What grudges won't go away? When does it rise above pettiness and show its best side? Who are its scapegoats and saviors?

Sarah Shepard's best-selling *Pretty Little Liars* (2006) is the start of a series about four girlfriends in an upscale prep academy, Rosewood Day School. Rich, spoiled, and a little mean, they're types familiar to young readers of the similar but more soapy series *Gossip Girl*. They dish, drink, smoke, shoplift, kiss girls, and sleep with teachers and their older sisters' boyfriends. They also take AP courses, run student council, excel at sports and raise money for charities. In short, they're perfect society bitches in training. Oh, and they're united by a dark secret referred to only as *The Jenna Thing*, and the eerie, vindictive return (via text) of a fifth friend who disappeared on the night of a seventh-grade slumber party. Quite a crew.

The liars might have been easy stereotypes, but their author is careful to make them both understandable and distinctive. She also takes some trouble to make specific the social world in which they live, that of Philadelphia's Main Line. It's a rich community, but not a McMansion farm.

Its Colonial-era homes with renovated barns and windmills, mown grass, and wood stoves, "old, noble bloodlines, older money and practically ancient scandals."

Early in the novel one of the liars, Spencer, who is locked in a rivalry with her sparkling older sister, Melissa, goes out for dinner with her parents to meet Melissa's new boyfriend. The restaurant is on a clipper ship in the Philadelphia harbor. As Spencer eats mussels, she contemplates her sister and her surroundings:

> The sisters had a quiet yet long-standing rivalry and Spencer was always losing: Spencer had won the Presidential Physical Fitness Award four times in elementary school; Melissa had won it five. Spencer got second place in the seventh-grade geography bee; Melissa got first. Spencer was on the yearbook staff, in all of the school plays, and was taking five AP classes this year; Melissa did all those things her junior year plus worked at their mother's horse farm and trained for the Philadelphia marathon for leukemia research. No matter how high Spencer's GPA was or how many extra-curriculars she smashed into her schedule, she never quite reached Melissa's level of perfection.
>
> Spencer picked up another mussel with her fingers and popped it into her mouth. Her dad loved this restaurant, with its dark wood paneling, thick oriental rugs, and the heady smells of butter, red wine, and salty air. Sitting among the masts and sails, it felt like you could jump right overboard into the harbor. Spencer gazed out across the Delaware River to the big bubbly aquarium in Camden, New Jersey. A giant party boat decorated with Christmas lights floated past them. Someone shot a yellow firework off the front deck. That boat was having way more fun than this one was having.

Notice two things about this passage: First, it uses specific details to bring alive Spencer's world of horse farms and heritage. Second, Spencer's relationship with her sister and her place in her social world are filtered through her unhappy feelings. Either details or emotions would be enough to sketch in Spencer's life, but the combination of both brings it fully alive.

What distinguishes our era? What are its look, buzzwords, issues, and conflicts? Fashion magazines, op-ed pages, sports reporting, rappers, corporate websites, and teen slang are all barometers of our times. Novels? Not so much. I don't mean to suggest dropping in brand names or news events. Those are shallow gimmicks. I do mean that an important component of any novel's grip on readers' imaginations is how that novel brings alive its times.

Historical novelists are often good at this. But how is a sense of historical era conveyed? It's conveyed through a character who lives in those times, which when you think about it is a great advantage. Strong opinions make strong reading. Just as we have opinions about our times, so characters do about theirs.

Amor Towles's novel *Rules of Civility* (2011) launched with a galaxy of starred reviews. A novel of society, manners, and fickle fortunes, it's set in Manhattan in 1938, the year that a Wall Street secretary's life and trajectory are transformed by a chance meeting in a Greenwich Village jazz club with a handsome but doomed banker. From a perspective of decades later, she sets the scene:

> I was sixteen when the Depression began, just old enough to have had all my dreams and expectations duped by the effortless glamour of the twenties. It was as if America launched the Depression just to teach Manhattan a lesson.
>
> After the Crash, you couldn't hear the bodies hitting the pavement, but there was a sort of communal gasp and then a stillness that fell over the city like snow. The lights flickered. The bands laid down their instruments and the crowds made quietly for the door.
>
> Then the prevailing winds shifted from west to east, blowing the dust of the Okies all the way back to Forty-second Street. It came in billowing clouds and settled over the newspaper stands

and park benches, shrouding the blessed and the damned just like the ashes in Pompeii. Suddenly, we had our own Joads—ill-clothed and beleaguered, trudging along the alleyways past the oil drum fires, past the shanties and flop-houses, under the spans of bridges, moving slowly but methodically toward inner Californias which were just as abject and unredeeming as the real thing. Poverty and powerlessness. Hunger and hopelessness. At least until the omen of war began to brighten our step.

Is this a narrator indifferent to her times? Is this the factual reportage of an historian? No. Towles's passage is shot full of bitterness, longing, and the rich recall of someone who was there, to whom the 1930s mattered. What of your own characters? How do they feel about the times in which they're living?

Contemporary novelists can be afraid of dating their novels with too many *au courant* cultural references, but I have news: It's impossible not to do so. Think about it. Novels published before the mid-1980s do not mention cell phones. How quaint! But nowadays what's a cell phone? A camera, a texting tool, a handheld computer running apps. Guess what? Twenty-five years from now all that is likely to seem quaint, too. So why worry? Indeed, the greatest classics are clearly of their age. Imagine *The Great Gatsby* without bootleg liquor or *To Kill a Mockingbird* without racism.

The mysteries of existence are also often avoided in manuscripts. Do you believe in destiny? Do you believe in God? Are our lives random or do they have a purpose? Do you think about these things? Of course you do. You don't just get up in the morning; you're a novelist. What about your protagonist? What's her take on the big questions? Is it pretentious to include them?

Ducking the big questions is easy. So is achieving low impact. See what I mean? If you think the biggest questions are only for Aristotle and Woody Allen, then consider that every sphere of human operation raises its own issues of cosmic significance. Is there such a thing as justice when laws are made by fallible humans? Does *do no harm* have any meaning when medicine becomes guesswork? Is it worth building bridges when their ultimate collapse is guaranteed? Do we teach in schools "truths" that are untrue? Does the accumulation of capital do good or does it corrupt? What are the limits of friendship? Should loyalty last beyond the grave? We read fiction not just for entertainment but for answers to those questions. So answer them.

Chris Cleave's international best-seller *Little Bee* (2008) tells the twin stories of a Nigerian refugee girl in the UK, known as "Little Bee," and the widowed mom, Sarah O'Rourke, editor of a glossy fashion magazine, who improbably becomes Little Bee's host and protector. (See chapter six for analysis of how Cleave makes this unlikely match-up credible.) Little Bee and Sarah are connected by an incident on a Nigerian beach in which Sarah chopped off her own middle finger in an unsuccessful attempt to save Little Bee and her sister Nkiruka ("Kindness"). For two years Sarah buries her feelings, but when Little Bee turns up at her door in suburban Kingston-upon-Thames, just days after Sarah's husband's suicide, Sarah can no longer avoid facing the meaning of what happened. Late in the novel she struggles to understand it, and the limits of her own responsibility, in a talk with her married lover, Lawrence:

> I looked out at the garden. The sky was darker now. It seemed the rain couldn't be far off.
>
> "Little Bee has changed me, Lawrence. I can't look at her without thinking how shallow my life is."
>
> "Sarah, you're talking absolute shit. We see the world's problems every day on television. Don't tell me this is the first time you've realized they're real. Don't tell me those people wouldn't swap lives with you if they could. Their lives are fucked up. But fucking up your life too? That isn't going to help them."
>
> "Well I'm not helping them now, am I?"
>
> "How could you possibly do more? You cut off a *finger* to save that girl. And now you're sheltering her. Food, lodging,

> solicitor . . . none of that comes cheap. You're taking down a good
> salary and you're spending it to help."
>
> "Ten percent. That's all I'm giving her. One finger in ten. Ten
> pounds in every hundred. Ten percent is hardly a wholehearted
> commitment."

Sarah's story makes us think, or it should. Are the world's problems really
our responsibility? What are we doing to help? Is it enough? How much
is enough? How much is too much? If you've ever felt guilt about not putting enough in the church collection plate, or felt that the checks you're
writing to charity are too small, then Sarah's situation is yours—except
writ large. Sarah gave more than any of us would reasonably do. And it's
not enough. Or is it?

Just as Sarah must grapple with the big issue of guilt, Little Bee must
find a way to move beyond her status as a victim. On a trip into London
with Sarah and Sarah's son, she sees a street entertainer disguised as a liz-
ard popping out of a box when coins are dropped in:

> But I saw it with my eyes. I saw the boy finally reach the big black
> box where the lizard man was hiding, and I saw him stretching
> on his toes to release the coin he was holding in his fist, and
> I saw the coin tumbling through the bright blue sky with the
> sunshine flashing upon it and the Queen of England's face upon
> the coin—with her lips moving and saying *Good Lord, we ap-*
> *pear to be falling*—and I saw the lizard man spring up out of his
> box and the boy run away giggling and screaming, and I saw
> his mother and father lift him up, and I saw the three of them
> hugging one another tight and laughing while the crowd looked
> and laughed with them. This I saw with my own eyes, and when
> I looked around the crowd I saw that there was more of it. There
> were people in that crowd, and strolling along the walkway, from
> all the different colors and nationalities of the earth. There were
> more races even than I recognized from the detention center. I
> stood with my back against the railings and my mouth open and

> I watched them walking past, more and more of them. And then
> I realized it. I said to myself, Little Bee, there is no *them*. This
> endless procession of people, walking along beside this great
> river, these people are *you*.

Before we leave this business of big issues, I'd like to give you a little test.
The following is a passage from a novel about the son of a pastry chef. Early in the story the narrator remembers the quality of his parents' relationship, and its effect on his life:

> Their love is deeper than desire, than affection, than respect, so
> deep that its wellspring is humor. Humor is a petal on the flower
> of hope, and hope blossoms on the vine of faith. They have faith
> in each other and faith that life has meaning, and from this faith
> comes their indefatigable good humor, which is their greatest gift
> to each other—and to me.
>
> I grew up in a home filled with laughter. Regardless of what
> happens to me in the days ahead, I will have had the laughter. And
> wonderful pastries.

Nice writing, would you agree? It's direct, emotional, and warm: plain
but beautifully written. It says something surprising about the wellspring
of humor, which is hope. Huh. This passage could comfortably sit in the
pages of any literary novel, but who wrote that passage? John Irving? Anne
Tyler? Someone with a lively, ironic voice? Actually it was the most commercial of thriller writers, a man with more than fifty smash best-sellers
to his credit: Dean Koontz. Read him and see. He has powerhouse plots,
a lively and ironic voice, as well as beautiful touches now and then that
wouldn't be out of place in literary fiction. (The passage above is from a
novel discussed in chapter six, *Life Expectancy*.) Maybe there's something
to this premise of mine?

Why not break down the social strata of your story world and make
sure there are characters who represent each? Why not worry less about

dating your novel and more about failing to capture its era? Why not identify and enhance the deeper issue that underlies the overt issue with which your protagonist is grappling?

The novel you are writing right now is your chance to say something of lasting value. Indeed, it's your opportunity to say something timelessly true. The highest impact of all is the significance and meaning of your story. Your readers want it. It's there. Find it and use it. Isn't it the biggest reason that you're writing?

⊷21ST CENTURY TOOLS⊷

PARALLELS, REVERSALS, AND SYMBOLS

- Pick anything that happens in your story. Create another event that's like it, or mirrors it. Add it.
- Find a dramatic event in your story. Create a smaller version of it for another spot in the story.
- Look at one of your protagonist's plot layers. Inflict an analogous problem on another character. Add it.
- What's something done by your antagonist or a secondary character? Find a place for your protagonist to do the very same thing.
- Or reverse the tool above: Have your antagonist or a secondary character mirror something done by your protagonist.
- How does your protagonist look at the main problem? How does it look different to her best friend? Add.
- Who sees things the same way that your protagonist does? What might happen to reverse that character's view? Make it happen.
- Send a gift to your protagonist. Make it huge, a windfall. What problem does it solve? What is its hidden cost? Add.
- Who or what is highly valuable to your protagonist? Take that away.
- What is your protagonist utterly, irrevocably right about? Pull the rug. Make her utterly wrong. List the implications. Enact each one.
- Elevate your protagonist's status. What privileges are awarded? What's dangerous about that?
- What's a moment when everything could change? Pause. Explore. What does it feel like to be weightless?
- Where is your protagonist heading right now? Shut down that road. Force a detour. What changes the most? How does your protagonist change as well?

- Do your protagonist's fortunes rise or fall? Pick a character whose fortunes will do the reverse. Develop and add.
- Choose a high moment in your story. Look around. Pick an object, one that's particular to this place, this moment, or these people. Now work backwards and forwards. Find at least three other spots in the story to plant this object.
- Find a corner, crossroads, or dark object in your story. Invest it with eeriness, unknown portent, or dread. Go there three times.
- Select a significant setting in your story. Find two other story events that also can happen there. Shift their settings.
- Pick a scene, maybe the one you're working on right now. Identify an emotion or idea, insight, or mystery that arises. Find a way to represent that physically. Broken phone? Squeaking windshield wipers? A ring too tight to remove?
- Write out your cast list. To each character assign an allegorical role: mother, destroyer, wanderer, sacrificial lamb, and so on. Now find one way for each character to more obviously enact their role. Add.

WORLD OF THE STORY

- List twenty things your protagonist notices in her story world that no one else does. Plant each somewhere in the manuscript.
- What's the most wonderful thing about the world of your story? Find two new spots to enjoy that.
- What's one unchanging feature of this story world? Observe it three times (protagonist POV or others). What's the mystery about it? Why is it holy?
- Take a minute. List three things about people that bug or intrigue you. How does your protagonist feel about each? Add.
- Take a minute. List three weird or wonderful things about your town. What are the equivalents in your protagonist's town? Add.

- Take a minute. List three bizarre or ironic things about society. Give them to your protagonist to notice.
- Take a minute. List five unbearable things about life. What could be fixed? What can only be endured? Give your protagonist those ideas.
- What's the opening mood in your story? Visualize it as an object. Describe it. What's most familiar about it? What's the most unexpected? Give that object to your protagonist to handle early in the manuscript. Bring it out again in your final chapter. How has it changed?
- For your story world, create a unique version of: sport, food, perfume or cologne, vehicle, vice, sin, festival, holiday tradition, flower or plant, remedy, coming-of-age rite, generation gap, courtship custom, death ritual. Add.

SURPRISE

- Pick a character. Drop a bomb. Destroy or transform his world. Nothing is as imagined. Everything is different. Work backward to make this character's foundations rock solid. Work forward to scatter the wreckage.
- Pick an ally of your protagonist. What's the worst betrayal this character could do? Do it. Work backwards. Make it something impossible to foresee.
- Pick an enemy. What's the most improbable way in which this enemy could help? Do it. Work backwards. Make it something impossible to imagine.
- You are God. Look lovingly down at your protagonist. What does she need? Give it. What does she need to learn? Teach the lesson. What do you feel like doing to your protagonist just because, hey, you're God? Do it.
- What's one thing your protagonist dearly hopes for? What would make that impossible? Do it. What does your protagonist get instead? Quietly plant that earlier.

- You're at the mercy of a puckish Story God. Pray. What do you ask the Story God not to do to your story? The Story God doesn't listen. What happens?
- Once you've unleashed a disaster upon your story, think through every implication. List every untidy consequence. What must be done to clean up the mess? That's your punch list. Work through it.

A SENSE OF SELF

- Look at your beginning. How does your protagonist understand himself? What defines him? What code or rules guide him? What assumptions are givens? What's home base? Who's on his side? In whose love is he secure? Who knows him as well as he knows himself? List all.
- Use the above list like this: At the end of your novel, how has the answer changed to any of the questions above? Shake those foundations along the way. What's needed to rebuild them? Add all.
- What's your protagonist's snapshot take on money, prayer, pop music, abstract art, minivans, modern dance, fourth-down passes, bespoke suits, raw food, blended whiskey, or anything else that demands an opinion?
- At the end of your novel, how has the answer changed to any of the questions above? What happens to change that opinion? Add it.

THE BIG PICTURE

- List the classes or social strata in your story world. Pick a character to represent each, its characteristics and values. Build and add.
- What's one unexpected or contradictory thing about each class? Embody each of those things in a character, too.
- Find three new times/ways for the classes to meet or clash.

- How does your protagonist feel about his place in his world? Find three spots to measure that, and how it's changing.
- What's the predominant philosophy in your protagonist's world? Imagine breakaway factions, hair-splitting denominations, opposing parties, or a revolutionary movement. Assign a character to one of those dissenting views. Show it one time in action.
- Give your protagonist a unique term for the story's era. What are three things about this era that your protagonist sees that others don't? What's the best thing about it? What's the worst? In what way is this era stuck? (Unstick it by the end!)
- How does your protagonist feel about the passage of time? Find three spots to measure that, its effect, and its changing feel.
- Is your protagonist in charge of his own destiny? If yes, show him that he's not. If no, show him that he is.
- What's your protagonist's conception of God? If she's humble, reward her. Is she's not, punish her.
- What's the cosmic question that your novel is addressing? Without stating it, how do the events of the story make it clear? Go further. Make that question, for the reader, inescapable.

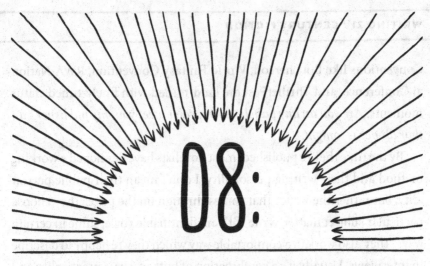

08:

THE 21ST CENTURY NOVELIST

PROCESS AND PERSONALITY

At the beginning of the learning curve, developing novelists are confused and uncertain. *Am I doing this right? Is it supposed to feel like this? How long will it take?* Later, there's an appetite for craft tips. How-to books, workshops, webinars, and study groups facilitate practical learning.

Still later, there arises a need for status checks. Advanced beginners start hanging around with published writers, attending conferences, and blogging. Scraps of validation take on high significance. Once, after presenting a workshop to a group of MFA students, I handed one of them my business card. At a party later, the student flashed the card around like it was a pass to an exclusive club. Other students expressed envy and anxiety.

As silly as that is, I see signs of status hunger at all levels of the writing game. When newbies land an agent, it's a big enough deal to be featured in their Twitter profiles. Published pros have their own way of bragging.

Conventions like Bouchercon, World Fantasy Convention, RWA National Conference, and ThrillerFest are land-mined with finely-tuned status moments. *Are you on any panels? Sorry, can't meet you, my publisher's author dinner is tonight.*

By the time they're published, most novelists have developed a working method and their writing personality. I don't mean their public personality, but rather the writer that comes through on the page. They choose particular subject matter, write with an identifiable voice, shine in certain ways. They also work in a comfortable way which they're happy to describe in interviews. Usually it's a combination of butt-in-chair practicality and magical obfuscation. *I write every day, it's all about discipline! I don't know how it happens, it just flows!*

I presume you have discipline. It's your writing methodology that interests me. Most authors stick to their programs. Whether elaborate formulae or a simple set of rules to follow, their working method serves. It's successful. It has resulted in publication and sometimes, later, in workshops and books of advice. When I attend those workshops and read those books, however, I find them alarmingly limited. Authors are good at explaining what they're good at, but not so adept at identifying what they do unconsciously or don't understand at all.

As a fiction writer you're naturally gifted at certain aspects of the art, but you're also lacking in others. You may be great at mile-a-minute plotting but slow to develop your characters' inner lives. Your manuscript may sparkle with glittery prose but lack long-lasting, thought-provoking themes. You may have command of a fleet of plot layers but not be so great at making each scene buoyant. Those lacks will blunt your power, not to mention your sales. It's wise to take a look at your working method and accept your strengths and weaknesses.

This may be the hardest chapter in this book to embrace. When it takes so long to break in, and it's so hard to break out, it's natural to stick to what works, take the shortest path, and play to your strengths. That's even more imperative once you are published. Not only have you crossed the big divide and reached the Promised Land, the stakes are now terribly high. Why experiment? Why risk? So much depends on keeping the wagon train rolling: your status, your self-respect, and probably even your mortgage.

Fortunately, working on what you're not good at yields both better fiction and greater success. Indeed, the most successful novelists I know are hungry students. They're not afraid to attend workshops. They treasure their critique partners and beta readers. They wait impatiently for their editors' revision letters, not to learn what they have to do to receive a check, but so they can make their novels better. They're smart and they're humble.

To write high-impact 21ˢᵗ century fiction, you need courage. Failure is possible, but the greater danger is not to try. With that in mind, let's look at the process of writing fiction from a couple of angles, and also give you a couple of simple writing personality tests. You'll see yourself in the pages ahead but also see the writer you're not. That's the writer you want to meet. It's the writer who's got what you're lacking and is your missing half.

OUTLINES VS. INTUITION

While we tend to think of commercial writers as outliners and literary types as the opposite, that's not necessarily true. I know puzzle-plot specialists who as they compose have no idea whodunit, and literary realists who extensively chart and map their manuscripts.

Neither type is pure. Outliners know their roadmaps can show only so much detail. At a certain point it's necessary to detour, guess, and improvise. Likewise, intuitive writers rarely explore terra incognita without some idea of where they want to go. They have markers to hit and scenes they know must be included.

Still, you're probably either an outliner or an organic writer (or *pantser*). Neither method is superior. Both are valid. Each has strengths and shortcomings. Outlines are highly efficient, but by their nature close off byways that could be fruitful to explore. Intuitive writing leaves possibilities wide open but can lead to aimless wandering. Outliners need freedom; pantsers need focus.

If you're an outliner, realize that you will outline what you understand and are good at. Of course, as you work, you'll hit holes in your plan. You'll hack through them. That's great, congrats, but you're still not getting out of your story everything that's available to enrich it. You need to push yourself into regions of your story world that you don't think you need to explore and into dimensions of your characters that take extra time to understand.

If you're an intuitionist, recognize that while you're unearthing mountains of rich ore, that's just a pile of rock until you refine it and shape it into steel beams that are then riveted into a framework. As you work, you likely nail certain moments. That's fabulous, but those gems are seductive. They're *so good*, yet preserving them can become an end in itself, almost an addiction.

If you are resistant to revision, recognize that your resistance is rooted in fear. If you are alarmed that your drafts are radically different, or if you never seem to be able to finish, start with this: Your novel definitely is about something, and that something is sharply defined, it's just that you're not yet letting yourself see and commit to it.

There are a lot of reasons for avoidance, but the cures boil down to one thing: Take a stand. Decide what's important, what hurts, what you know that your readers don't, what it is that people (including your characters) urgently need to *see*. That's your missing focus, the refining fire that will turn the ore into steel.

You may not think you know those things, but I am positive you do. There are things important to you. You hurt. You know stuff I don't. You see things that I cannot. If I'm wrong about that, then you might possibly be dead, but I doubt that, too. You have everything you need, including the courage to declare your story's intent.

Outliners and intuitionists may have opposite lacks, but their solutions are the same. The shortcomings of both approaches to novel writing are best overcome not by trying to be something you're not but by believing in yourself, your story, and your ability to own and enjoy the fullness of your gifts as a novelist.

RESEARCH VS. OBSERVATION

Do you research your novels to the point of obsession, or do you not research at all?

Historical novelists are research junkies. Coming-of-age novelists mostly rely on memory. The majority of fiction writers fall somewhere in between: They study just enough so that their settings are accurate and their characters' occupations feel real. The rest is *write what you know.*

There's nothing wrong with that, it's just that heavily researched novels can be lacking observation of the ordinary. Conversely, realistic novels are frequently too ordinary to be fascinating.

To create high impact, it's necessary to both observe people as they are and to discover through research that which readers could not possibly know about them and their world. Don't you love learning new stuff as you read? Don't you also love it when you totally recognize the characters with whom you're spending time?

Research means not just getting the setting details right. It means getting the people right. Have you met a character who was shot with a bullet but wasn't psychologically changed? Ever run across a protagonist who adapted to his handicap, special gift, or paranormal ability with no trouble whatsoever? Those are failures of research.

Failure to observe people as they are results in overly familiar characters, actions, and emotions; that is, stereotypes, predictable events, and hackneyed prose. It's a paradox. When you write what you think you should, it doesn't feel wholly real. When you write from life, characters become quirky and unique.

There's another dimension of research that's often overlooked: working out the logic of one's story events. Just as science-fiction writers work out the logic of their speculative worlds, all novelists need to determine whether the events in their story could really happen in the way that they're written. If you're an oncologist, novels probably are spoiled for you when the author screws up the details of chemotherapy. As a kid I was a competitive sailor. In novels that involve sailing vessels, I can always tell when authors are faking it. (The word "rope" is a dead giveaway; sailors don't use it.) Sometimes the logic to be worked out is even simpler than that.

While I don't necessarily recommend studying readers' comments on Amazon.com, it's sometimes instructive to check out what's said by those who give the lowest rankings to successful novels. Kazuo Ishiguro is a winner of the Whitbread Prize and the Man Booker Prize, among other honors. In his novel *Never Let Me Go* (2005), he borrowed an idea long familiar to science fiction fans: (big spoiler here) cloning. The children at British boarding academy Hailsham are unaware, but gradually learn, that they are clones bred to donate their organs and die early. The novel doesn't question how this came about but instead focuses on a love triangle that poignantly plays out as its members undergo their fate.

Never Let Me Go was a critical success, was made into a movie, and thrilled hundreds of Amazon reviewers. Those who did not like it, however, had one universal complaint: The premise is ridiculous! No one objects to organ harvesting? The clones do not revolt or simply blend into society? Ishiguro's saying that clones are human, yet the clones lack an instinct for self-preservation? One reviewer commented wryly, "This book might be interesting if you've never read a science fiction book before." Perhaps it doesn't matter, and no doubt Ishiguro's purpose was to create a metaphor for the human condition, but his story's logic is lacking.

If you're naturally an observer, undertake some research to make your story distinctively detailed and imaginatively rich. If you're a dedicated researcher, get your nose out of the books and notice people. It's what you uniquely observe about them that will make your characters real. Whichever type you are, make sure that what happens in your story is psychologically authentic and factually credible. While you can't fool all of the readers all of the time, it's a good idea to fool most of them as much as you can.

DEADLINES VS. SPEC

Do you love deadlines or hate them? Are you happiest when you've got a multiple book contract, or when there's no pressure to deliver?

Most commercial novelists, unless they deliberately avoid them, work under contract constraints, meaning deadlines. It's not always comfortable. I know this from the number of times I have to ask my clients' editors for delivery extensions. On the other hand, the freedom of working without a deadline can be counter-productive. I know this because there are clients who can disappear for years. They're usually working steadily, just not finishing anything.

There's a school of thought that says writing fiction needn't be slow. Indeed, if you get out of your own way, you can produce novels at astonishing speeds. National Novel Writing Month (NaNoWriMo) and boot camp workshops taught by my friends Kristine Kathryn Rusch and Dean Wesley Smith are founded on that principle. The results have shown conclusively that the unconscious mind writes faster than fingers can type. Quality may be debatable, but speed is an indisputable fact.

You either thrive under pressure or you don't. Whatever your preference, it's best not to fight it. On the other hand, it's a good idea to recognize the problems that your way of working brings. Novelists under contract tend to meet their deadlines, but just barely. There usually isn't time for extra development, let alone exploration or experiment. Commercial storytellers on a book-a-year pace, in fact, often are turning in first drafts: slick, mind you, but exactly as outlined and lacking surprise.

Novels written without duress may result in stories of wider scope, with interesting side trips and full of lovely surprise. They can also be messy, sprawling, unfocused, and slow in spots. (They can equally be small in scope, too short, and frustratingly lightweight.) Freedom doesn't always make a story stronger. It can instead allow a novelist to avoid big decisions and hide from the hard parts.

If you are a pressure lover, your need is to build into your process time to deepen your characters and explore your story's hidden potential. If you don't have time for that, early in the process take time to pose to yourself a few of the simple questions at the end of this chapter. They're designed to give you at least a couple of ideas you would otherwise not be able to execute. It's worth doing. The time involved may be small, and the extra pages few, but the impact will be big.

There's value in getting lost once in a while. You never know what you might find. At the same time, when there isn't a map, it's important to have a vision, a clear purpose, or a firm intent to compass-point you to the powerfully magnetic novel that's inside you. Your comfort zone is not a safe place—not if you want to be a high-impact 21st century novelist. Step out of it and step into a world of possibilities that will make you a stronger writer.

COOL VS. WARM

Here's a question for you: Who's the superior writer, Jane Austen or Ernest Hemingway? If you answered Jane Austen, then you probably write more emotionally, embracing exposition and characters' interior lives. If you answered Ernest Hemingway, then you may believe that emotions on the page are cheap, gooey, and artless. For you, showing rather than telling is not just good advice but an iron law.

Restraint, showing, suggestion, and subtext all are valid fiction techniques that lie on the cool end of the spectrum. They're most pronounced in the kind of literary fiction that's called minimalist, but coolness is a quality that can prevail in any type of story. Cool writing can excite admiration, but it acts to distance readers from characters. In its extreme form it reports a story at arm's length.

Interiority, exposition, reactive passages, and emotional exploration are techniques that fall on the warm end of the spectrum. They're most noticeable in romance novels and women's fiction but can be found in plenty of literary novels as well. Warm writing invites readers' emotional involvement but leaves less room for readers' imaginations. When you supply everything readers are supposed to feel, they may wind up feeling little at all.

Cool writers can benefit from warming up to their characters and opening their interior lives. Warm writers can become stronger storytellers by more often showing through action, using restraint, and suggesting feelings rather than slathering them on.

Sandra Brown is one of our most versatile and dependable novelists. Skilled in many forms, in 2009 she took a break from the women's suspense on which she's been focusing and brought out *Rainwater*, a Depression-era story set in Gilead, Texas. Ella Barron runs a boardinghouse and does her best to manage her mentally handicapped son, Solly, whom we later learn may be an idiot savant. At the request of the town doctor she takes in a new boarder, David Rainwater, who has come to quiet Gilead to die.

Rainwater asks little but slowly begins to break through the walls of routine and emotional distance that has kept Ella isolated. Meanwhile, racism and corruption run rampant in Gilead. Rainwater gets involved. When a local black minister is lynched, a violent confrontation and climax is set in motion. But as tense as that is, equally tense is the struggle between Ella and Rainwater. He is trying to get through to her. She resists.

One night a storm sweeps through and Ella closes the storm shutters. Rainwater is up, too. Tension crackles between them, but Brown plays it with understatement:

Ella knew she must look as disheveled as he, maybe more so. Her hair was wildly curling around her face, a tangled mane down her back. Her robe was damp from the rain. The wet hem of it clung to her ankles. Her feet felt cold and clammy, reminding her she was barefoot.

All this registered with her in a matter of seconds, during which it seemed to her that her breath had been snatched from her body. A lightning bolt struck dangerously close. The thunder that followed shook the house. Glassware and china made tinkling sounds inside cabinetry. The light fixture above the hallway rattled. The back door slammed, echoing the thunderclap.

Even then, neither of them moved. Their eyes stayed locked. Ella's heart felt on the verge of bursting.

She said hoarsely, "The storm finally broke."

He held her stare for several moments longer, slowly shaking his head. "No. It didn't."

She drew in a tremulous breath, her heart crowding her lungs, and forced her feet to move.

Ah, delicious. Not even the heavy-handed lightning and overused romance words like "tremulous" take away from the tingling erotic current. Brown lets locked eyes and a simple double-entendre do the job. Less is more. Showing is better than telling. Or to put it differently, Brown builds the heat by playing it cool.

Just as warm writing can wake us up with a burst of cool water, cool stories can unexpectedly warm us up. What about a story about racial tensions in a small English village? Let's construct it around a Montague-Capulet romance: In this case a proper Englishman and a Pakistani immigrant woman. Such a story probably ought to be written with spare emotions and tremendous restraint, wouldn't you say? I mean, this is England. And it's a serious subject, deserving a serious style. It sounds like an Ian McEwan novel.

But it's not. *Major Pettigrew's Last Stand* (2010) by Helen Simonson, a *New York Times* best-seller, is the story I'm describing, and it's about as warm and charming as a literary novel can be. You could dismiss it as cutsie, cozy, and false, but Simonson's eye is accurate and the prejudices of seaside Edgecombe St. Mary are too ugly to be so easily brushed aside. At any rate, a huge number of readers found this novel thought-provoking and memorable. How can that be, when its tone is so gentle and sweet?

Let's take a look at one of Simonson's snuggly passages and see if we can discern why readers have taken her story seriously. The novel's protagonist is a retired army major, Ernest Pettigrew. Early on, his brother dies. Soon after that, Pettigrew is given a lift in the car of his London-based son and daughter-in-law. (The son was too busy with a billion-dollar bond deal to attend his uncle's funeral.) Pettigrew rides in the back seat and drifts:

> The Major said nothing. He relaxed his head against the leather seat and gave himself up to the soothing vibrations of the road. He felt like a child again as he dozed and listened to Roger and Sandy talking together in low voices. They might have been his parents, their soft voices fading in and out, as they drove the long miles home from his boarding school for the holidays.
>
> They had always made a point of coming to pick him up, while most of the other boys took the train. They thought it made them good parents, and besides, the headmaster always held a lovely reception for the parents who came, mostly ones who lived nearby. His parents loved the mingling and were always jubilant if they managed to secure an invitation to Sunday luncheon at some grand house. Leaving late in the afternoon, sleepy with roast beef and trifle, they had to drive long into the night to get home. He would fall asleep in the back. No matter how angry he was at them for sticking him with lunch at the home of some boy who was equally eager to be free of such obligations, he always found the trip soothing; the dark, the glow of the headlamps tunneling a road, his parents' voices held low so as not to disturb him. It always felt like love.

Hoo-boy, does it get much cozier than that? *Soothing, lovely, sleepy, roast beef* . . . the very words convey comfort. So, is this passage just a bowl of trifle? You no doubt have noticed my contempt for the three Rs of inactive literary writing: reaction, reflection, and remembering. Isn't that also exactly what this passage is, in spades? On the surface, sure. But look deeper. What's the hidden tension? Pettigrew is old, his too-busy son is distant. Looking back to the sleepy, back-seat car trips home from boarding school with his parents, the major remembers feeling loved. Which, by implication, he isn't now. In other words, while this car drive may feel warm and cozy it's actually conveying Pettigrew's longing for something he's missing in his life; which also serves later to make credible his attraction to a widowed Pakistani shopkeeper who adores literature.

Warmth and literary intent are not mutually exclusive. Whatever your natural temperature as a writer, it's good to be aware, acknowledge the limitations of your propensity and, selectively, work to compensate. When your coolness is balanced by warmth, and your warmth at times is restrained, your fiction will broaden in appeal. Readers of every inclination will find in it something to enjoy.

MY BABY VS. MY BUSINESS

We've all met her, or even been her: The author who cries upon receiving a rejection or revision letter. The writer who's got a million reasons not to change what she's written. *It's the way I see it! I don't control my characters; they take over the story!* Or my favorite excuse: *That's how it actually happened!*

In the industry we tend to dismiss such attitudes as amateurish and celebrate writers who evidence the reverse: *I'm easy to work with because I love to revise! I treat my writing as a business!* A certain detachment is without a doubt a good thing, but so is passionate conviction. Are they in opposition? I don't think so. Just as it's silly not to revise, it's equally destructive to buckle too readily. Swaying to the tune that others think you should be playing doesn't make your music great.

The most pressure I see put on writers are in the fields of romance and Christian fiction. Publishers in these areas are extremely twitchy over readers' sensitivities. In fact, it's rare to meet long-published romance or Christian novelists who don't want to break free of their categories. They've had to constrain themselves for too long. On the other hand, I sometimes think that established literary novelists are tested too little. Paid high respect, they are under-challenged and too easily stumble.

What's the right balance? How do you know when to take advice and when to stick to your guns? You know you're fallible as a writer but, damn it, this is your story and it's your name on the cover. And then there's the reverse problem: *My editor thinks my manuscript is almost perfect. She hardly asked for any changes at all!*

I've seen a lot of editorial fights. In fact, sometimes I think that instead of an agent's black suit I should wear a referee's black-and-white uniform. Mostly both sides have a point. The author's gone too far in some way, such as realistic effect: sex needlessly explicit or violence that's sickening. But on the other hand the editor's being too cautious. Compromise is needed. That's what I usually counsel and usually it works.

The time to stick to your guns is when a change would not just change your manuscript but demolish your plot or lobotomize your protagonist. In the heat of the moment it can be hard to tell the difference. Be honest with yourself. Is what you're hearing truly plot demolition and character assassination, or simply a change you're resisting for other reasons? (Like, *I need that check!*)

The toughest resistance comes when an author feels that a requested change will gut his style or soften his story's intent. That's rarely true. Think about it. How often have you heard a reader say, "I'm quitting that author! He doesn't use enough four letter words!" Or, "I wish she had hammered her point harder!" Agents and editors are first readers, and while they can occasionally be wrong, they also are experienced. Their job in part is to articulate what bookstore consumers will feel when it's too late.

If you get an offensive editorial e-mail, take a day to cool off and think. It's common for authors to report, "I hated my editor when I got that e-mail, but she was right." Once in a while I have had to intervene and read the Copyright Act to a publisher, but not terribly often. There's a way to accomplish your purpose with a story in a way that works for many readers, I promise.

The more difficult task, I think, is to create in your manuscript character moments and story events that make you question even yourself. Most often authors play it safe. So here's your challenge: Go too far. Or fear that you have. The stuff you invent that makes you uneasy, if not nervous, may be just the stuff that makes your next novel your best ever. Timid storytelling may be good enough to get published, but only strong and courageous story gambits will create high-impact 21ˢᵗ century fiction.

ENTERTAINMENT VS. TRUTH

What's more important to you, entertaining your readers or revealing the truth of things? Both? Maybe, but your writing itself will tell me on which side of that divide your values predominantly lie.

Entertainers often are unashamed. The harder they insist on their purpose, though, the more likely it is that I will find their stories formulaic and their characters stereotypical. The truth tellers, by the same token, can be equally uncompromising. Yet the more they avow their disdain for commercial success, the more I know I will find their manuscripts small and chicken-hearted.

Each group is avoiding what they're not good at. Entertainers need to please the crowd less. Truth tellers need to embrace story more.

If you're writing in a commercial category, you're living in a familiar house. Its structure is pleasing and its nooks are cozy. You've dwelt there so long you don't see the dust in the corners and you tolerate the fluky water heater. Hey, it's your home. And that's the problem. You've grown accustomed to its flaws and even insist that they're part of what gives your house its charm.

If you're blazing a trail and don't give a damn what anyone thinks of that, you might be ahead of your time but you might also be precluding failure by rejecting success. Isn't it better to be misunderstood, outcast, impoverished, and suffering? Isn't that a prerequisite of creating art? Well, I disagree. A few great novelists were obscure in their time; Herman Melville, say. But not too many. A small group of novelists have been appreciated more after their death. Philip K. Dick is an example.

The truth is that most of the novelists we revere today were in their own time either commercial or critical successes, or both. Timeless stories mostly are appreciated in their age. Regardless, you want your stories to have impact. You want them to move people, if not change them. You want to be read. What makes that possible are characters to whom readers can open themselves and stories that dramatize the truths you know. You have to connect, but to connect you have to work at what makes that connection.

To write high-impact 21ˢᵗ century fiction you don't need to entertain, but you do need to be accessible. You don't need to discover original truths but you do need to write in a way that is personal. Entertainment and truth are not polar opposites. Story is stronger when it brings insights, and insights sink in when they're enacted through stories. Whether your purpose is to illuminate or entertain, you can make your fiction more effective by doing more of the other.

PLEASING VS. GROWTH

What's more important to you, satisfying your fans or growing as a writer? If fans complain, do you lie awake at night or merely shrug? When your editor suggests a story change you don't agree with, do you rush to revise, think about it, or fire back a grumpy "stet"?

Pre-published fiction writers would love to have this issue. Long-published pros can tell you, though, that success can be a golden coffin. Fans, once your friends, can turn into tyrants. Editors, once your champions, can be afraid to kill the profit center.

What can you do when the need to please runs up against your need to grow, stretch, test your limits, and learn new ways to tell your stories? It's a tough spot to be in. It usually results in a fight, which unfortunately means someone must win and someone must lose.

It needn't be like that. Satisfying fans is good. So is growth. The two can be complementary. The way to marry them is to first identify why you feel that you want to change. Many of the fights I've witnessed between authors and their editors have had their roots in weariness. Years of hitting tight deadlines takes its toll. After a while authors begin to resent working so hard.

Boredom can be a factor, too. At some point this almost inevitably sets in with romance and series authors. They rebel, but mostly it's because they've been doing the same thing for too long. They haven't taken risks. It's not their series or story form that's at fault; it's the authors' own failure to set challenges.

The hardest factor to counteract is financial pressure. Sometimes the rebellious impulse comes not from a creative need but from worry. Sales are off. Income has suffered. Change is needed, sure enough, but a radical change of direction is not going to solve the problem. Indeed, it's likely to make the problem worse. What's needed instead is stronger storytelling, whatever the form.

Once you know why you feel the need to grow, you can plan to do it. If repeated deadline pressure has got you down, ease up. Even the most hardened agents and editors understand the danger of burnout. I recently got a publisher to agree to give a best-selling client a year-long break. This happened even as a huge new contract was in the works. Fortunately the publisher is human and knew that her profit center is human, too. Fans might grow impatient, but, honestly, they'll wait. And be rewarded.

If boredom is your reason for rebellion, a wholly new type of novel might be right, but that's not usually the case. A simple shake up might be enough. Fans may howl when you kill off a beloved series character—or worse, a fuzzy pet—but I've never seen that destroy a series.

If you write standalone novels, set yourself a challenge. Experiment with a new tense, person, or point of view. Rattle or reverse some of your assumptions about your characters or their course of action. Sticking with what's easy and what you've already got will keep you stuck in a rut. The cure for boredom is being bold.

If money worries are making you restless, realize that the fundamental problem is not creative but financial. Creative revolutions can be refreshing but they're not a guaranteed route to fiscal security. The best way to judge whether a change of direction is the right result for you is to first factor out the money worry. What if you had a lucky lottery win? What would you write? Ah. There you go. And that is what you should be writing anyway.

The best plan of all is to build growth into every novel you write. In each new novel, top sellers typically try to top themselves. What's a challenge *you* can set in your current work in progress? Set it and meet it. I will bet that when you succeed you won't meet resistance, but rather garner praise. Experiments aren't experiments when they work. They're risks taken and richly paid off, most of all in the new skill you've learned and the satisfaction you feel in writing at your best.

➤ 21ST CENTURY TOOLS ➤

OUTLINES VS. INTUITION

- Are you an outline writer? Take an afternoon off. Take a walk. Bring a notebook and pen. Ask, "If a gutsier novelist than me were writing my book, what would happen in the story that isn't happening now?" Ah.

- Are you an outline writer? Take your protagonist out for coffee. Ask, "Something's bothering you . . . is there something you'd like to tell me?" Listen.

- Are you an outline writer? Take a slow walk through the world of your story. No rush. Notice one thing that you didn't see before. Find a way to use it.

- Are you an outline writer? Plan a side story to offer as a freebie prior to publication, such as a detour with a secondary character or a dropped plot thread. Now, does this really have to be an extra? Can it go into the manuscript?

- Are you an intuitionist? Burn your manuscript. Erase your hard drive and your back-ups too. Phew. Feel better? Now, in fifteen minutes write down what you really want to say.

- Are you an intuitionist? You have superhero vision. What do you see that no one else does?

- Are you an intuitionist? You have godlike perspective. So tell us . . . what do people get wrong? How are they supposed to act, but don't? What's the point of life? What's the meaning of creation itself? Work through every scene in your novel until each answers one of those questions.

- Are you an intuitionist? You run a crisis hotline. The phone is ringing. It's your main character. She's in distress. She needs to know what to do. You're trained not to say "wait" or "do nothing." That doesn't work. What do you tell her to do?

RESEARCH VS. OBSERVATION

- Are you a researcher? Go to a public place. (Not the library!) People watch. Pick up one weird detail. What's something odd, ironic, or interesting about people in general? Make a note. Use that in your story.
- Are you a researcher? Think about your family. What kind of people are they? Who's best? Who's worst? Who's the coolest? Who's the nastiest? How? Use that.
- Are you a researcher? Read the newspaper. What's the big issue nowadays? What's the equivalent issue in your story? Strengthen it.
- Are you a researcher? What's something ironic about life? Give that ironic observation to one of your characters. Better still, show it happening.
- Are you an observer? What's your protagonist's occupation or identity? Interview someone who's got that job or profile. Ask, "What do outsiders not know? What's something you feel that others don't? What's a specialist term, tool, or measurement you use that others don't?" Use that stuff.
- Are you an observer? Invent something for your story world that doesn't exist there. Make it something big, notable, colorful, creepy, mysterious, famous, singular, or a source of shame or pride or wonder. Put it in your story.
- Are you an observer? Pick a secondary character. Give that character an extraordinary ability or notorious past. Find a way for that to cause something to happen.
- Are you an observer? What could happen in your story but doesn't because it would be a stretch? So . . . stretch. Work out how it would happen. What would have to be different? Make it different. Make it happen.

DEADLINES VS. SPEC

- Are you on a deadline? When you reach the halfway mark in your first draft, pause. Ask, "What's the step I'm afraid to take for this story? What would pump it up to giant size?" Go there. There's still time.

- Are you on a deadline? Take two minutes, no more, to quiz your protagonist: Who really bugs you? What would you like to say or do to that person? Give permission. Go for it.

- Are you on a deadline? Pull aside a secondary character. Ask, "Are you frustrated? What would you like to do in this novel that you're not able to?" Give 'em the chance. Do it.

- Are you on a deadline? Guess what? Your story's weak. It's not saying what you want it to say. What's the biggest thing you can do in one afternoon to guarantee that your story will sing out? Guess what? The Story God's feeling good. You've got that afternoon. Use it.

- Are you a spec writer? Write the one-day version of your novel. Yep. Whole novel. One day. What happens on the page? That's your core story.

- Can you do that? Write the one-hour version of your novel. That's your one- or two-page synopsis.

- Are you a spec writer? When you finish your next draft, turn into the bitch editor from hell. Send yourself a revision letter. Make it hurt. Make it on target. Hit every weakness, every cheat. Give yourself sixty days to revise.

- Are you a spec writer? You're hiding from something in your story. What is it? Face it. Use it.

- Whether you like deadlines or not, what's the biggest thing you're afraid to do in your current novel? Try it. It could be the most important thing you're missing.

COOL VS. WARM

- Are you a cool stylist? What scene are you working on right now? Who's your point-of-view character? Open a fresh document. For fifteen minutes let your POV character spew what she's feeling. Is any of that useful in the scene?

· Are you a warm writer? What scene are you working on right now? Who's the POV character? Pause. Ask that character, "Hey, how would you like to act out here? Go on. Go crazy." Given permission, how does that character go gonzo?

· Are you a cool stylist? What's your main character not saying right now? Have another character say it instead.

· Are you a warm writer? What's your main character feeling in your latest interior passage? Make your main character suddenly reticent. Convey the feeling solely through action.

BABY VS. BUSINESS

· Is your book your baby? Look at your current scene. Cut 200 words. Fail? Cut 500.

· Is your book your baby? Look at your main character. He's a jerk. Make him shape up in one big way. Right now. No excuses.

· Is your book your baby? You've gone too far. You haven't gone far enough. Which is it? Guess what? It's the opposite of what you think. You have work to do. You know that's true. Make a list of the top five weaknesses. Get to it.

· Are you all business? What's your favorite moment in your current manuscript? Disaster! Your editor says cut it. Don't argue. Don't justify. Revise until your editor has to cave.

· Are you all business? Make your protagonist do something that will piss off your readers. Too bad, readers, live with it.

· Are you all business? What's your novel saying that people won't want to hear? Buy yourself billboard space next to a busy highway. Splash that message. Make motorists mad. Now make that message as hard to miss in your manuscript.

ENTERTAINMENT VS. TRUTH

· Are you an entertainer? Your story has in it one huge, hoary cliché. You know that's true. Find it. Kill it.

· Are you an entertainer? There's a character in your story who is a big, fat stereotype. Don't deny it. Fix it.

· Are you an entertainer? There's one way in which you're going too easy on your protagonist. You're not fooling anyone. Go on. Make things tougher. Make them horrible.

· Are you a truth teller? What's a truism that's too common to allow into your novel? Go ahead and say it, or let a character say it.

· Are you a truth teller? What's a feeling too saccharine to abide? Satisfy your sweet tooth. Use it. Don't worry about calories. The rest of your story is rigorous exercise.

· Are you a truth teller? What's a gimmick too cheap and cheesy to use? You're right. It's a gimmick. But what's a variation that could work for you? Ah.

PLEASING VS. GROWTH

· Do you write a series? Change a series character. Violate a series rule. Do something that will mean things can never be the same. Feels good, doesn't it?

· Bored with your story? What story development would make you happy? What are you waiting for?

· You won the lottery! Congrats. You can ditch your manuscript and write what you want. What is that? Well? Write it.

· Burning out? Phone your agent. E-mail your editor. Take a break. Take away pressure. When you return, take a fresh look. Why were you stuck? Try a different approach. There's probably less wrong than you fear.

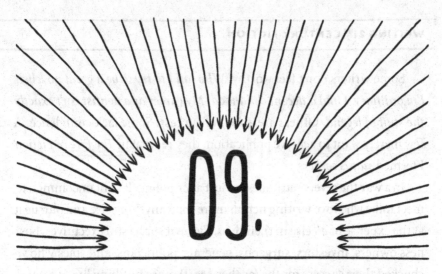

09:

THE ELEMENTS OF AWE

FEAR

Have you ever read a novel all too predictable, one that's just okay, or one that's similar to a bunch of others out there? Did you ever find yourself mentally griping to an author, *Oh, don't tell me that's where you're taking this story! Seriously, no!* Are there some novels you've found easy to purge from your shelves?

By contrast, do you have novels in your collection that are keepers, the ones you never lend out? Are there novels that you remember years later or re-read regularly? Do certain authors dazzle you with almost every outing? Do you pray, "Lord, let me write as well as that author, just for one manuscript! Even for just one day!"?

Which author would you rather be, the throw-away or the keeper? I'm pretty sure of your answer, so let's talk about how to become that writer. Let's start with what's holding you back.

Some writers don't feel worthy. *Who am I to try to be a great novelist? I'm ordinary. I had a decent childhood. My career as a dentist isn't exactly the stuff of legend.* Others are afraid of success. Some lack confidence. A few merely want to achieve publication; they're what in *The Fire in Fiction* I termed *status seekers.*

In a way the reverse attitudes are just as crippling. It's not uncommon to meet folks who love writing fiction more than anything else and pursue it at the expense of *all* else in their lives. I've met successful executives, business owners, investors, surgeons, generals, politicians, and spies who've chucked their success for the (as they see it) more fulfilling life of a novelist. (About the only professions I've never run across in the ranks of newbies are billionaires and professional athletes.)

The problem with these overconfident writers isn't that they're afraid, but that they're fearless. Already successful in one field, they imagine that success at fiction writing is just a matter of application. Take the right courses, work with the right independent editor, invest a year or two, and you can nail this fiction business. One such writer I met at a workshop asked me midway through, "What's my take-away? What's the one thing I need to know?"

Wow, wrong questions, as I'm sure you can easily see. Whether suffering from underconfidence or overconfidence, too many fiction writers don't make it to publication and too few who do graduate out of the minor leagues. Nothing says you have to be a best-seller or write an ageless classic, yet too many novels leave me, like you, feeling underwhelmed, malnourished, or empty.

It's a shame when novels achieve less than they could. As I read I often wonder what the author is afraid of. Do deadlines (real or self-inflicted) cut short the creative journey, or are there paths in the woods that the storyteller fears to walk? The rush to publish certainly is a factor. It's sad to see hurried third volumes in trilogies, say, rushed into production by overworked editors. But I don't think that's the whole story. After all, novels are built day by day in writing sessions that can be either comfortable or courageous.

I believe in sending characters down fearful paths. Stories pushed beyond the limits of comfort stick in readers' imaginations. That's an effect most novelists want to have. But that means living with worry. What if you've gone too far? What if your editor—worse still, readers—are turned off? And, heck, pushing a protagonist to dangerous places and painful states of mind is emotionally exhausting. Who wants to live that way?

On the other hand, consider this paradox: When other novelists unsettle us, we praise them, yet when in our own writing we unsettle ourselves, we worry.

That's weird.

And backwards.

Can we turn that around? Can we turn our fears to our advantage?

I believe so. In fact, it's imperative if you're going to write high-impact 21st century fiction.

What gives a story high impact is that which is most personal and passionate in its author. That includes your own fears. They are your compass. They're pointing you to what unsettles. And also to what matters.

At the end of this chapter are tools to help you focus on your protagonist's fears, and your own. The object is to turn them into story. So use them. Fear is your friend. Open your door. Invite fear in. Smoke cigars. Have a chat. What you're afraid of may be just what you need.

FIREWORKS

Chances are that last Fourth of July you saw fireworks. Pasteboard tubes soared into the dark sky, erupting in sizzling blooms of strontium, lithium, calcium, sodium, barium, copper, cesium, potassium, rubidium, iron, aluminum. Spectators gasped, surprised every time.

Chances are that sometime recently you also read a manuscript or novel that launched few fireworks at all. Instead you encountered black words lined up in endless rows, an army of safety attacking on tiptoe and retreating without a shot. Colors seemed washed out. Characters felt bloodless, dead. A whole novel went by and no one had anything to eat?

Why is it that when fireworks slash open the night we cheer, yet as we tenderly arrange our words across a white screen we fear drawing blood? Maybe that'd be messy. Perhaps we hate calling attention to ourselves.

Too many manuscripts tell their stories with timidity. What's needed instead are explosive bursts of divinity: explosions of insight, booms of self-revelation, scenes that flare open in the dark, prose that sizzles like sparklers. How can we light those fuses? There's hidden gunpowder in every dialogue exchange, every event, every exit. Your main characters can douse themselves in gasoline. Secondary characters can throw Molotov cocktails. You are a god hurling thunderbolts. Or you can be. All it takes is taking delight in shaking things up.

We love fireworks, yet we hate to set them off. We're happy when others dazzle us but don't feel entitled to do the same. Sometimes the shells explode by accident, of course. We're happy when they do. But how often do we send up fireworks by design? Generally speaking, not often.

To write high-impact 21ˢᵗ century fiction, setting off fireworks by design is exactly what must be done. The prompts at the end of this chapter are designed to help you do that whenever you want to, which I hope will be often. So do it. Do it for you. Do it for me. The night is long. The hours of darkness are dull. We need more fireworks. Set them off on purpose and like Fourth of July spectators, we'll be surprised every time.

THE ELEMENTS OF AWE

Who spreads stories and why? Sociologists at the University of Pennsylvania have been studying data provided by *The New York Times* showing which of the paper's articles are the most often e-mailed. Their conclusions are important for fiction writers because they reveal what it is in stories that generates word of mouth.

The first element is one that will be obvious to most of us, so let's cover it right away. Positive articles are e-mailed more often than negative ones. What does that mean for novelists? It means that excitement is more likely to be stirred by characters with positive qualities and by stories with happy endings.

No big surprise, like I said. If your characters are dark, miserable, and self-loathing, you can't expect readers to be enthusiastic. Qualities of strength, especially when we see them right away, inspire readers to care. Downer endings also narrow a novel's appeal. But you already knew that, right? Right.

The next element identified by researchers is a little harder to appropriate. More frequently e-mailed stories tend to be emotional.

Stop. I know exactly what you're thinking. *All riiight! My novel-in-progress is highly emotional! Best-seller list here I come!* Not so fast. Every author thinks his or her novel is packed with emotion. Naturally they do. As they write, they feel tons of emotion. But that is not to say that those emotions are getting through to readers, or in ways that move readers deeply.

What's the strongest emotion that your protagonist feels: anger, disgust, shame, betrayal, terror, frustration, elation, arousal, love? Yawn. Sorry, not feeling it. Here's the point: You can't expect your readers to feel what your protagonist feels *just because your protagonist feels it*. Only when that emotion is provoked through the circumstances of the story will your readers feel what you want them to.

Describing sorrow is fine, but not as effective as your protagonist saying goodbye to her dying mother . . . and even that is not as good as saying goodbye after a rich experience of mother-daughter love . . . and even *that* is not as good as if that love was hard won. *Welcome home* is another heart grabber, but only when it seems like it will never happen. In other words, emotions aren't gold. A story situation that provokes strong emotions is.

Surprise is another element that causes folks to share stories they've read. Intriguing facts, unexpected puzzles, people who aren't what you at first expect them to be . . . all those are surprising; what we sometimes call *hooks* in openings. But hooks will only take you so far. Their effect is momentary. Novels are long.

Large scale is another key element. In fiction terms, that comes from multiple points of view richly rendered and a story that doesn't stint. Tales of war, epic quests, and the like are by nature large scale, but that doesn't mean they clobber readers with their grandeur. It takes more than that. Fully explored themes, multi-step character journeys, nuanced social strata, profound changes, and contrast in a cast of characters are needed to truly create a feeling of scale. In fact, those elements can convey that sense of scale even when a setting is contained or a timeframe is limited.

The most important factor in provoking readers to spread the word about a story is an effect that the Penn researchers call "awe." This they defined as an "emotion of self-transcendence, a feeling of admiration and elevation in the face of something greater than the self." It demands of readers "mental accommodation," meaning readers must see the world in ways they didn't before.

Dr. Jonah Berger and Dr. Katherine Milkman, authors of the study, further explained that the effect of awe can come from "the revelation of something profound and important in something you may have once seen as ordinary or routine, or seeing a causal connection between important things and seemingly remote causes."

That academic mouthful describes what great fiction does: It creates characters we become, brings us into their experience, and makes it real. It then reveals to us through their inner journeys and themes what it all means. Stories become relevant when they're highly different than our own. Strange worlds strangely become ours. Singular problems become universal conflicts. What's murky becomes lucid. Great fiction opens readers' hearts and, once they're captive and pliant, opens readers' minds.

To open readers' minds, you've got to have something to open their minds *to*. This is where high-impact 21st century fiction gets personal. It's made of characters only you can create, events only you can devise, settings brought alive as you see them, changes wrought in ways you understand, connections you alone perceive, secrets and mysteries you ache to unlock, and a perception of things so persuasive that it becomes your reader's way of looking at things, too.

You can't borrow awe. You can't plot it into existence. You can't provoke it through pretty words. It has to come from you. Your fiction will be awesome to the extent that you cut loose from convention, go to places that belong to you alone, and embrace your godlike inner storyteller. How? Bond me to your characters. Put them through a fearsome story. Force me to feel what they feel. Show me how they change. Finally, make me see things your way.

If you think about it, aren't the people who've had the most influence on you the ones who caused you to look at things in a new light? Bingo. Be that novelist. And you can, now that you know how.

21ST CENTURY SUCCESS

It's funny what some authors think of as success. A big advance, best-seller status, and starred reviews all are common feel-good tokens, but one time I worked with an author who had all that in abundance yet was miserable. Why? He's never been asked to be guest-of-honor at a genre convention. He seriously asked me how to go about getting such an invitation, which he felt was his due.

I long ago grew weary of such misplaced emphasis, but I also realize that fiction writers are human. Validation, especially in a field so competitive and chancy, is a natural need. It's also balanced by an exceptional level of sharing and community. Fiction writers are some of the most connected and generous folks I know. Writing used to be a lonely profession. Not anymore.

Despite all the rich information and social opportunities available to novelists, especially online, certain topics are never discussed. For instance, failure. The status of "published" is permanent. No amount of poor sales, dropped options, unreturned calls, or withering reviews seems to tell novelists that change is needed. If there's any change at all it's usually a change of agents.

That's a shame. What's worse is that I can often see failure coming. You can too, I'll bet, though it's impolitic to say so. The pages of published novels are chock full of poorly developed stories, stereotypical characters, lazy prose choices, haste, and failure of nerve. Have you ever given up on a once-favorite writer? Guess what? Your readers do the same thing but with far less guilt.

The seeds of failure are sown on the page; or perhaps more accurately, the seeds of success are *not* sown there. In fact, I'll go further: Success or failure is inherent not just in the stories you write, but in the way you engage in the process, the values you bring to your fiction, and your very notion of success.

It's a truism of query letters that those who claim to have written best-sellers never have. Authors whose goals are material are focusing in a way that will make it hard to get the rewards they seek. Industry legends about calculated best-sellers don't help. Every John Grisham or Nicholas Sparks who is said to have cynically set out to write a best-seller fuels that mythology. It suggests that commercial success is a grubby plan while literary success is the opposite, an unearned gift of genius.

Neither notion is true. Commercial and literary success both are the result of hard work, instinct, study, and a steady honing of craft. They're not mutually exclusive. As I've argued all the way through this book, strong storytelling and beautiful writing are the twin elements that make a big and lasting impression on readers. Those who embrace both values succeed. Art and craft are not the same thing, but one without the other will surely produce inferior novels and probably long-term failure.

What is success in the 21st century? It's novels that invent their own unique form, spring from a personal place, enact a passionate intent, and prove it by reaching a broad readership. It's both great reviews and great sales. It's moving hearts and changing minds. It's winning accolades and winning the devotion of readers. It's finding a way through your fiction to convey what you alone see, yet we all come to accept as the truth.

Can 21st century success be measured in royalties? I don't think so, but it frequently is. It's not uncommon for high-impact fiction to be listed, lauded, hand-sold in bookstores, adopted by book clubs, and made into movies. It reaches across demographic lines and does so, paradoxically, by telling stories that couldn't happen to just anyone or be written by anyone but that author.

Success is built on all that we've studied in these pages: standout characters, the marriage of inner and outer journeys, beautiful writing, and the contradictory union of structure and improvisation. Authors who succeed in the 21st century honor the best of their literary antecedents but also lead a revolution. They're of their time and they're timeless. They're comfortable with discomfort. Their values as novelists lie not in any external measures of validation but in the inward quest for vision, voice, and made-up worlds that are more vividly real than reality itself.

Success in the 21st century is engaging in a process that demands the utmost of oneself. It requires embracing fear, exploding fireworks, and diving into those aspects of character and story that are uncomfortable. It means taking a hard look at the writer you are and a harder look at the writer you're not. That brave engagement brings rewards. You'll feel them long before your agent and editor praise you, long before the starred reviews, far ahead of the film options, in advance of the awards, and sooner than the royalty statements that affirm your stellar sales.

You'll feel your success as you write. Beyond your commitment, above your hard work, you'll see yourself tackle something you thought was impossible and pull it off. You'll make story choices that scare you to death but fill you with life. You'll know that there's a message in your heart that readers will hear. You'll bring alive a world that never will die. You'll be writing better than you ever dreamed. You will know without having to ask, or be told, that your life's purpose is fulfilled.

Welcome to the 21st century. The old ways of storytelling have much we can borrow. But it's what you make new that will make you singular and successful. Aim for a marriage of great story and beautiful writing. That degree of impact is not just for a lucky few. It's something you can achieve, too. And you will.

There's a 21st century novelist inside you. When you set that writer free, you may not only write a novel that defines our times, but one that lives on through the ages. Set that goal and you have your eyes on the success I'm talking about. In fact, you're there already.

❧ 21ˢᵀ CENTURY TOOLS ❧

FEAR

- What is your protagonist's deepest fear? What is its origin? Triple the magnitude of that event.
- What is your protagonist's deepest fear? Rehearse it or brush up against it twice. Then bring it about.
- What is your protagonist afraid to confess or admit to himself? Bring him up against it, big time. Make it impossible to avoid.
- Earlier in life, what was your protagonist's worst mistake? Make it even worse. Now find a way to bring that event into the present. If it's a secret, bring it to light. Who is hurt? Make it hurt more.
- What's your own deepest shame? What do you most regret? What have you ruined? What have you lost that you will never get back? What are you powerless to change? Give any of that to your protagonist.

FIREWORKS

- Pick a scene at random. What does your protagonist really want to say? What's the most blunt, rude, or raw way in which she can say it? Make her use those words. Let the wreckage fall.
- What's an event that passes with little notice? Invent a dire consequence. Make it one that no one sees coming. Who or what can be wrecked? What is the worst outcome of that disaster? Get those in.
- Choose a character with little to do. Create for her a gift to give. Make it a gift that will transform the recipient. Give that gift at the time of greatest need.

   Set off fireworks between two characters. What's the biggest skyrocket you can explode for the finale? Go ahead . . . *kaboom!*

- Select an entrance or exit. Dress it up, make it dance onto (or off) the stage. Work with its effect on your point-of-view character. What will he (or we) never forget?
- Choose a scene involving violence or sex. Create an action that we don't expect. What deep wound is opened? What unexpected joy arises? What is the irrevocable truth now known?
- Turn to any page in your manuscript. Pick a sentence that's just quietly doing its job. Pump it full of speed. Make it hallucinate. Include a word from poetry. Find in it something sublime, if not divine. Make it explode.

THE ELEMENTS OF AWE

- Look at your first chapter. Put in something positive. Don't worry. We'll survive.
- What's one way in which your protagonist is hopeful? How quickly can you get that in?
- What is the strongest emotion you want your reader to feel? What event will provoke that emotion the most? This is your story's signature moment. Find three ways to heighten the effect you're shooting for.
- ADD: an intriguing fact, a tough puzzle, a character who is not what he first seems to be.
- ADD: a different take, an alternate outcome, an opposing belief, an extra mystery.
- ADD: a character from a different social strata, a symbol of these times, a harbinger of the future, a sign from God.
- If your story sprawls, plant something small, personal, and domestic at the beginning. Bring it back at the end.
- If your story is tight, what is its cosmic meaning? Choose a character (other than your protagonist) who sees that.
- Your protagonist changes: Is it a change we all need to make? Make it more so.

- What does your story explain? Work backwards. Make the mystery deeper, the solution harder to see.
- Think about the last year: What do you see differently than you did one year ago? Get that in your story.
- List your life lessons. Now . . . well, you know what to do.

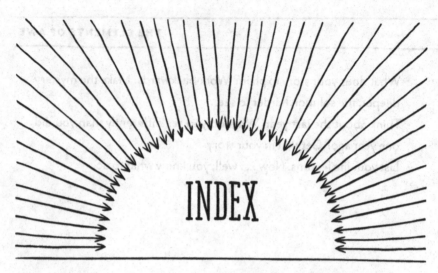

INDEX